MEANING AND THE ENGLISH VERB

Geoffrey N. Leech

Professor of Linguistics and Modern English Language
University of Lancaster

LONGMAN

Longman Group Limited
London

*Associated companies, branches and representatives
throughout the world*

© Longman Group Limited 1971

First published 1971
Fifth impression 1976

ISBN 0 582 52214 5

Printed in Hong Kong by
Dai Nippon Printing Co (H.K.) Ltd

Contents

55974

iii

Acknowledgements

I am very grateful

to Valerie Adams for reading through and commenting on the earlier chapters of this book

to Sidney Greenbaum not only for chapter-by-chapter comments, but for kindly undertaking research on American English

to R. A. Close, for a careful reading of the manuscript with a particular eye to the needs of the foreign learner

to Paul James Portland (of the University of Wisconsin) for detailed observations from the point of view of the speaker of American English

University of Lancaster   GNL

Key to Symbols

$'will$:

The bar $'$ indicates that the following syllable is stressed.

★*It has rained tomorrow*:

The asterisk indicates an unacceptable or 'non-English' utterance.

Simple Present:

The initial capitals indicate a grammatical category.

'possibility':

The quotation marks indicate a semantic category.

AE: American English
BE: British English

Introduction

1 Every language has its peculiar problems of meaning for the foreign learner; and most people would agree that in the English language, the most troublesome problems are concentrated in the area of the finite verb phrase, and include, in particular, questions of tense, aspect, and modal auxiliary usage. The object of this book is to describe such fields of usage systematically and in some detail for teachers and advanced students of English as a second language, or for that matter, for anyone interested in the subtle workings of the English language.

Much – some might say, too much – has already been written on the semantics of tense, aspect, and modality in modern English. Some of the most perceptive as well as the most useful treatments are to be found in course books such as W. Stannard Allen's *Living English Structure*. Recent more scholarly accounts have made important contributions at a specialist academic level (they include Robert L. Allen's *The Verb System of Present-Day American English* and Madeline Ehrman's *The Meaning of the Modals in Present-Day American English* in the U.S.A., and F. R. Palmer's *A Linguistic Study of the English Verb* in Great Britain). A third group of writers – those of the 'orthodox' grammatical tradition represented by Poutsma, Kruisinga, and Jespersen – remains the most plentiful source of detailed and well-documented information, as well as much insight on the subject.[1]

2 Why, then, this book? Because, in my opinion (and in the opinion of foreign students and teachers with whom I have discussed these matters) there is still a need for a book which co-ordinates and makes more accessible what can be learned from the literature just mentioned, systematically explaining the semantics of the English finite verbal phrase in a way unencumbered by discussions of syntax and morphology, and in a way which presupposes no specialist interest in linguistics. Furthermore, I have tried to rethink the subject in the light of developments in semantics over the past few years: developments which have resulted in a sharpening of tools for the analysis of meaning.[2] It is my hope, therefore, that whatever is new in the approach I take will help readers not just to learn facts, but to co-ordinate and deepen their grasp of the language, by seeing facts (wherever possible) not as isolated facts, but in a fresh way, as part of a regular pattern. I should like them to see generalisations where none

55974

were evident before, and perhaps to recognise that the English language is less 'illogical' and wayward than they may previously have thought. This is not to say that exceptional usages or 'irregularities' can be ignored, and much of the space within these covers is devoted to the task of accounting for them.

While stressing what is new in this book, I should also like to acknowledge what is old – that is, the extent to which I have drawn (as anyone writing in this field cannot fail to draw) on the extensive literature I have referred to above. I have avoided placing acknowledgements in the chapters of description, in the belief that this would merely distract attention from the task in hand. But this obliges me here to make clear my general indebtedness to others, and to point out that a Guide to Further Reading, with brief comments (pp. 123–126) gives a more precise indication of how this study is founded upon those of previous writers.

3 As this volume, basically speaking, is concerned with a set of grammatical forms in relation to a set of meanings, a reader might expect a presentation which works from the forms to the meanings like this:

CHAPTER 1 Meanings of the Present Tense
CHAPTER 2 Meanings of the Past Tense
CHAPTER 3 Meanings of the Perfect Aspect . . .

or else one that works from the meanings to the forms, like this:

CHAPTER 1 Ways of expressing past time
CHAPTER 2 Ways of expressing present time
CHAPTER 3 Ways of expressing future time . . .

In fact, I have found it convenient (since in any case there is continual need for reference back and forth from one section to another) to adopt a combination of these two approaches, grouping observations now according to form and now according to meaning. For example, Chapter 1 'Simple Present and Past Tenses' takes grammatical forms as its point of departure, while Chapter 4 'The Expression of Future Time', starts from meaning. What is lost in consistency here is, I feel, atoned for by the flexibility which makes it possible to bring together contrasts and similarities in whatever seems to be the most illuminating way. At the same time, for convenience of reference, there are summaries at the beginning of all chapters, and a full index at the end of the book.

4 In discussing the relation between grammar and meaning, one is faced not only with problems of lay-out, but with problems of terminology. Most of the grammatical categories that have to be discussed (Present Tense, Perfect Aspect, etc.) have labels which are derived from a characteristic feature of meaning, but which can be very misleading if they are used as if semantic rather than grammatical labels. It is a notorious fact, for instance, that the English Present Tense can refer not just to present time, but to past and future time as well. To overcome this difficulty, I have made use of a typographical convention whereby grammatical categories are marked by initial capitals (Present Tense, etc.) to distinguish them from corresponding categories of meaning or reference (present time, etc.). Where necessary, single quotation marks are used to indicate citation of meaning rather than form. Thus the following arrangement:

Lightning can be dangerous ('It is possible for lightning to be dangerous')

represents a semantic gloss on a sentence identified formally.

Grammatical terminology has been chosen solely with the goal of immediate intelligibility in mind. The term 'tense' is used not only for the primary distinction of Present Tense and Past Tense, but also for the sub-categories Present Perfect Tense, Past Progressive Tense, etc. The term 'Aspect' is reserved for the primary categories of Perfect and Progressive modification. In case terms are not found to be self-evident, the following may be given as a tabular guide to the grammatical nomenclature of the first three chapters:

	(non-progressive)	Progressive Aspect
(non-perfect)	Simple Present Tense *he sees*	(ordinary) Present Progressive Tense *he is seeing*
	Simple Past Tense *he saw*	(ordinary) Past Progressive Tense *he was seeing*
Perfect Aspect	(ordinary) Present Perfect Tense *he has seen*	Present Perfect Progressive Tense *he has been seeing*
	(ordinary) Past Perfect Tense *he had seen*	Past Perfect Progressive Tense *he had been seeing*

As the table shows, the expressions 'non-perfect', 'non-progressive' and 'ordinary' are used (wherever necessary) to denote forms unmarked for one aspect or the other. 'Simple' is used of forms unmarked for both aspects.

5   The type of English I am mainly concerned to describe may be called 'contemporary standard British English'. But discrepancies between American and British English, as well as variations of style, are noted where they are important. Dialect variation in verbal usage has been little investigated, but it appears that there are considerable differences, especially in the use of the modal auxiliaries, within Great Britain and the U.S.A., and even between different age—groups. This book therefore necessarily simplifies a rather complex picture, did the labels 'BE' (British English) and 'AE' (American English) can at best be regarded as showing *typical* usage in their respective countries. For information about the English language, I have resorted mainly to introspection into my own command of the language, a procedure which has disadvantages, but which has the one supreme advantage of being practical. Similarly, the examples I use are invented rather than borrowed from texts, as it is of great value in this kind of study to have simple, self-explanatory, economical illustrations. However, the fact that this study has been read in manuscript by a number of native speakers of English has provided a check of my own observations.

NOTES

[1] See the Guide to Further Reading, pp. 123–126.
[2] In particular, I have in mind the use of paraphrase, ambiguity, and acceptability as tests for investigating contrasts and similarities of cognitive meaning. Modern theoretical approaches to semantics lay stress on such concepts: see Jerrold J. Katz and Jerry A. Fodor, 'The Structure of a Semantic Theory', *Language*, Vol. 39 (1963), pp. 170–210. A study of more direct bearing on the present one is Geoffrey N. Leech, *Towards a Semantic Description of English*, London: Longman, 1969, (esp. Chs. 1, 7 and 9).

One

Simple Present and Past Tenses

6   In all the uses of the Present Tense there is a basic association with the present moment of time (the moment of speech). This association can be expressed as follows: 'The state or event has *psychological* being at the present moment'. This element of meaning does not (as we see in §§ 14–17) exclude the possibility of its having *actual* being at a time other than the present. The Present Tense in special circumstances can refer to past and to future time exclusive of present time: in the 'historic present', it represents past events *as if* they were happening now; in the 'future present', it refers to future events regarded as *already predetermined*.

We may fittingly start, however, with the more usual application of the Present Tense to present time – limiting discussion in this chapter to the Simple Present Tense.

SIMPLE PRESENT: UNRESTRICTIVE USE

7   The UNRESTRICTIVE use of the Simple Present is found with verbs expressing states. It is so called because it places no limitation on the extension of the state into past and future time:

Honesty *is* the best policy. | War *solves* no problems. | How many languages *does* he know? | We *live* in London.

However, limits to the duration of the state may be implied by an adverbial expression which underlines the 'presentness' of the period in question, so indicating a contrast with some other period:

Crime is the best policy *these days*. | War *no longer* solves any problems. | *At present* we live in London.

a. ★*We live here since 1950* and ★*We live here for twenty years* are incorrect because the phrases *since 1950* and *for twenty years* identify a period of time leading up to the present moment. The perfect tense is appropriate in these cases: *We* HAVE LIVED *here since 1950/for twenty years* (see § 55).

8   The Simple Present is suitable for employment in the expression of 'eternal truths', and so is found in scientific, mathematical and other statements made 'for all time':

Hydrogen *is* the lightest element. | Two and three *make* five.

Not surprisingly, it is also characteristic of proverbs:

Necessity *is* the mother of invention. | A rolling stone *gathers* no moss.

Geographical statements are likewise, for practical purposes, without time limit:

Rome *stands* on the River Tiber. | The Atlantic Ocean *separates* the New World from the Old.

These usages follow from the definition of the unrestrictive use of the Present in § 7.

SIMPLE PRESENT: INSTANTANEOUS USE

9   The INSTANTANEOUS use of the Simple Present contrasts with the unrestrictive use in that it occurs with verbs expressing events, not states. It signifies an event simultaneous with the present moment, and normally occurs only in certain easily definable contexts; for example

In sports commentaries: Napier *passes* the ball to Attwater, who *heads* it straight into the goal! | Walker *swings* a right at the West Indian—he *ducks* and it *glances* harmlessly off his shoulder.

In the patter or commentary of conjurors and demonstrators: Look, I *take* this card from the pack and *place* it under the handkerchief—so. | Now I *put* the cake-mixture into this bowl and *add* a drop of vanilla essence.

In most of these cases, the event probably does not take place *exactly* at the instant when it is mentioned: it is subjective rather than objective simultaneity that is conveyed.

10   We may compare the following as two ways of describing the same action:

I *open* the cage. | I *am opening* the cage.

The second sentence, which contains a Progressive verb form, is a neutral description in answer to the question *What are you doing?* But the first sentence is rather dramatic, because it insists on the total enactment of the event as it is reported: if spoken, one would expect it to be accompanied by a gestural flourish; in writing, it seems incomplete without an exclamation mark. The instantaneous use of the Present also occurs in exclamations like *Here* COMES *the train!* and *Up we* GO! It is generally the 'marked' or abnormal alternative to the Progressive Present, because there are few circumstances in which it is reasonable to regard an action as begun and completed at the very moment of speech.

a. The theatrical quality of the instantaneous present is affirmed in its employment in old-fashioned stage rhetoric (now chiefly used in comic parodies): *The bell tolls! He yields! The spectre vanishes!* etc.

b. It is significant that there is no instantaneous present question form *What do you do?* comparing with the frequently-heard question *What are you doing?* This is presumably because by the time an instantaneous action has been noted and queried it is already in the past, whereas the Progressive allows for a time lag.

11   Less dramatically, the instantaneous use is found in asseverations such as *I beg your pardon*. Here the event and the act of speech are simultaneous simply because they are identical; that is, the thing announced and the act of announcement are one. Other everyday examples are:

We *accept* your offer. | I *dare* you to tell him that! | I *deny* your charge. | I *say* that you are wrong.

These PERFORMATIVE VERBS express formal acts of declaration, in contrast to the Progressive forms *We are accepting your offer*, etc., which merely report the speaker's present activities or future intentions. This usage is also characteristic of more ceremonial contexts, such as

ship-launching: 'I *name* this ship . . .'
judge passing sentence: 'I *sentence* you to . . .'
card and board games: 'I *bid* two clubs.' | 'I *resign*.' | 'I *pass*.'
wills: 'I *bequeath* . . .'

a. The declarative acts discussed here do not include superficially similar expressions of wishes and condolences such as *We wish you every success* and *I send you my deepest sympathy*. These belong rather to the category of cognitive states (§ 37F). The distinguishing marks of declarative acts are (1) that they are almost invariably in the first person, and (2) that they permit the insertion of *hereby* in front of the verb.

STATES AND EVENTS

12 The contrast between STATES and EVENTS has already appeared as the foundation of the distinction between the unrestrictive and instantaneous uses of the Simple Present. It is time now to consider this contrast more carefully.

The choice between 'state' and 'event' is inherent in all verbal usage in English. A state is undifferentiated and lacking in defined limits. An event, on the other hand, has a beginning and an end; it can be viewed as a whole entity, and can also make up one member of a sequence or plurality of happenings.

The difference between the two is parallel to that between countable nouns (those that can be made plural, such as *house/houses*) and mass nouns (those that cannot be made plural, such as *milk*). The division in nouns, however, is more clear-cut, because it is grammatically indicated by the plural ending. There are no such indicators of 'event' status in the verbal phrase. What is more, nouns (with the possible exception of words like *cake*) must be normally placed in one class or the other; whereas verbs are generally neutral, and capable of switching from 'state' to 'event' or *vice versa*.

In fact, to speak more plainly, 'state' and 'event' are semantic rather than grammatical terms. Strictly, we should not talk of 'state verbs' and 'event verbs', but rather of 'state' and 'event' meanings or uses of verbs. It would be inconvenient, however, to avoid the expressions 'state verb' and 'event verb' altogether. These useful labels are retained here, but it must always be remembered that they are *convenient labels*, for what would be more precisely designated 'verb being used to refer to an event/a state'. We may take the verb *remember* as an example:

> Suddenly I *remembered* the letter. | I *shall remember* that moment until I die.

In the first sentence *remember*, because it refers to the act of recall, is an 'event verb'; in the second it is a 'state verb', representing the notion of 'having in one's memory'. (Quotation marks will always be used with these two labels, as a reminder of their provisional status.)

The following are among the verbs normally used as 'STATE VERBS':

be, live, belong, last, like, stand, know, have, contain.

The following is a selection of verbs normally acting as 'EVENT VERBS':

jump, nod, get, put, land, begin, find, hit, fall, go.

It must not be supposed that these are the only two categories; some other types of verbal function ('activity verbs', 'process verbs', etc.) are considered later, in §§ 36–8.

SIMPLE PRESENT: HABITUAL USE

13 A third use of the Simple Present, that of the HABITUAL or ITERATIVE USE, is like the instantaneous use, confined to 'event verbs'. In fact, its relation to the instantaneous present is analogous to the relation of a plural to a singular noun. The habitual present represents a series of individual *events* which as a whole make up a *state* stretching back into the past and forward into the future. It thus combines aspects of the instantaneous and unrestrictive uses:

> He *walks* to work. | I *buy* my shirts at Harrods. | Whenever ammonia *is added*, the colour *changes* to orange. | He who *hesitates* is lost.

As the last two examples show, the habitual resembles the unrestrictive present in its suitability for 'eternal truths' of a scientific or proverbial nature. To emphasise the element of repetition and universality in these two sentences, one might paraphrase them *On every occasion when ammonia is added* . . . and *Every time someone hesitates, he is lost.*

As a way of interpreting 'event' verbs, the habitual present is more common than the instantaneous present, which, as we saw in §9, is rarely found outside a few limited contexts. Many verbs more or less have to be taken in an iterative sense, because the event they describe takes far too long to be envisaged as happening singly and once-and-for-all, within the moment of speech. *He walks to work*, for example, makes one think of an established habit (a series of repeated events), not just of a single event. In fact, few sentences are ambiguous in this respect. Sometimes a plural object helps to single out the habitual meaning:

> He scores *a goal*. (instantaneous use)
> He scores *goals*.   (habitual use)

On other occasions, an adverbial expression of frequency reinforces the notion of repetition:

> I *generally/often/sometimes* buy shirts at Harrods. | He cycles to work *most days/twice a week/every day*.

Hence, even when the verb permits both instantaneous and habitual interpretations, some other linguistic indication of iteration is frequently supplied.

SIMPLE PRESENT REFERRING TO PAST AND FUTURE

14   In addition to these three uses with reference to present time (i.e. time including the present moment), the Simple Present may refer to FUTURE TIME exclusive of the present:

> I *start* work next week. | The train *leaves* at eight o'clock tomorrow.

This use is discussed in relation to other means of indicating future time in §§ 101–4.

15   Also the Present Tense may be used in reference to the past. The use traditionally known by the term HISTORIC PRESENT is best treated as a story-teller's licence, whereby past happenings are portrayed or imagined *as if* they were going on at the present time. It is most evident where the Present Tense is accompanied, with apparent incongruity, by an adverbial expression indicating past time:

At that moment in *comes* a messenger from the Head Office, telling me the boss *wants* to see me in a hurry. | Last week I'*m* in the sitting-room with the wife, when this chap next door *staggers* past and in a drunken fit *throws* a brick through our window.

Such utterances are typical of a highly-coloured popular style of oral narrative, a style one would be more likely to overhear in the public bar of a village inn than in the lounge of an expensive hotel.

A distinction may be made between the strict historic present described here, and the use of the Present to narrate fictional events (see § 25).

16 A different kind of historic present is found with 'verbs of communication' in such sentences as:

Joan *tells* me you're getting a new car. | (in the correspondence column of a newspaper or journal) Your correspondent A.D. *writes* in the issue of February 1st that . . . | The ten o'clock news *says* that it's going to be cold. | We *learn* in the Book of Genesis that all differences of language originated in the Tower of Babel. | I *hear* poor old Mrs. Baxter has lost her cat.

The verbs *tell*, *write*, and *say* here refer to the initiation of a message in the past; therefore we have reason to expect the Past or Perfect Tenses: *Joan has told me* . . .; *The ten o'clock news said* . . .; etc. However, it appears that the verbal meaning has been transferred from the initiating end to the receiving end of the message. The communication is still in force for those who have received it, and so the Present Tense is allowed. In a sense, the Book of Genesis, although written over 2,500 years ago, 'speaks' at the present time: its message is still there for whoever wants to avail himself of it. Verbs like *learn* and *hear*, which refer to the receiving of the message, here refer rather to the state of *having received* the message. Thus *I hear Mrs. Baxter has lost her cat* can be replaced, with little change of effect, by *I understand* (= 'I have the information') *that Mrs. Baxter has lost her cat*.

17 The following sentences illustrate a similar extension of the Present Tense to cover information which in strict historical terms belongs to the past:

In THE BROTHERS KARAMAZOV, Dostoevsky *draws* his characters from sources deep in the Russian soil, not from fashionable types of his day. | Like Rubens, Watteau *is able* to convey an impression of warm, living flesh by the merest whiff of colour.

When discussing an artist and his surviving work, one feels justified in using the Present, because the work, and through it (in a sense) the artist, are still 'alive'. The whole career of a painter, writer, or musician may, in fact, be viewed as a timeless reconstruction from the works themselves. Here there is almost free variation of Past and Present Tenses. The sole difference between *Brahms* IS *the last great representative of German classicism* and *Brahms* WAS *the last great representative of German classicism* is a difference of point of view: i.e. whether one prefers to think of Brahms as a composer still living through his compositions, or as a man who died in the nineteenth century. Subject to § 17*c*, however, we do not have this choice in dealing with the purely biographical details of an artist's life: the Present Tense cannot be substituted for the Past Tense in *Brahms* WAS BORN *in Hamburg*; *Brahms* COMPLETED *his first symphony in 1876*; *Brahms* SPENT *the last 35 years of his life in Vienna*.

a. Free variation between Past and Present Tenses occurs additionally in cross-references from one part of a book to another: *The problem* WAS/IS *discussed in Chapter Two above*. For cross-references to a later part of a book, a similar free variation exists between Present and Future: *We* RETURN/SHALL RETURN *to this topic in the next chapter*. The author has the choice of whether to see his book as a whole artefact existing at the present moment (so that what is written on page 2 is just as much in present time as what is written on page 300); or to see it on a shifting time scale, from the point of view of a reader who reaches page 2 'before' he reaches page 300.

b. In newspaper headlines, the Simple Present is preferred (perhaps because of its brevity) to the Past or Perfect Tenses as a way of announcing recent events: *Ex-champ dies*, a headline reporting the death of a former boxer, contrasts with the Past Tense that one meets in the corresponding prose account: *Bill Turton, one-time holder of the British welter-weight championship,* DIED *at his home in Chesterfield yesterday*. The 'headlinese' use of the Present Tense has something of the dramatic quality of the 'instantaneous present' (see § 9).

c. Two minor uses of the 'historic present' are (1) in photographic captions (*Father O'Brien gives his first blessing*); and (2) in historical summaries, tables of dates, etc.: 1876 – *Brahms finishes his first symphony*.

SIMPLE PAST: NORMAL USE
IN REFERENCE TO PAST TIME

18   There are two elements of meaning involved in the commonest use of the Past Tense.

One basic element of meaning is: 'the happening takes place before the present moment'. This means that the present moment is excluded: *I lived in Sicily for ten years* (as opposed to *I have lived in Sicily for ten years*) makes it clear that I no longer live there.

Another element of meaning is: 'the speaker has a definite time in mind'. This specific time in the past is characteristically named by an adverbial expression accompanying the Past Tense verb:

Haydn was born *in 1732*. | *Once* this town was a beauty spot. | We visited Selfridges *last week*.

Both these aspects of Past Tense meaning are more fully discussed in connection with the Perfect Tenses in §§ 61, 63–4.

19   With the Past Tense, the difference between 'state' and 'event' is less significant than it is with the Present Tense. Indeed, as the Past Tense applies only to completed happenings, everything it refers to is in a sense an 'event', an episode seen as a total entity. There is nothing in the past corresponding to an indefinitely extensive present state, insofar as whole lifetimes or even whole eras of civilisation may, in historical retrospect, appear as complete, unitary happenings:

William Barnes *was born*, *lived*, and *died* in his beloved county of Dorset. | The water of the Nile *sustained* the prosperity of the Pharaohs for thousands of years.

Thus for the Simple Past Tense, there is no clear-cut contrast between 'event' and 'state' uses, corresponding to that between the instantaneous and unrestrictive presents. There is, however, a distinction to be drawn between the unitary past and the HABITUAL PAST, describing a repeated event (cf. § 13); an example of the latter is *In those days I enjoyed a game of tennis*.

20   There is also a contrast between past events happening SIMULTANEOUSLY and past events happening IN SEQUENCE.

He *enjoyed* and *admired* the sonnets of Petrarch. | He *addressed* and *sealed* the envelope.

The first sentence does not alter its meaning if the order of verbs is reversed (='He admired and enjoyed . . .'); but an alteration of the order of verbs in the second sentence suggests an alteration of the order in which the actions took place: *He sealed and addressed the envelope* usually means something different. Sometimes, as in *He shaved and listened to the radio*, it is not clear whether the happenings are meant to be at the same time or one after the other. When the happenings have only a brief duration, however, it is more natural to regard them as stages in a sequence, especially in narrative contexts.

a. Other temporal relations between two consecutive Past Tense forms are possible if overtly signalled by a conjunction or adverbial expression, or if made clear by our knowledge of historical precedence: *Their party* CAME *in sight of the mountain top three hours after ours actually* REACHED *it;* likewise (comparing the maritime achievements of Phoenicia and Portugal) *The Portuguese* LIVED *on the fringes of Mediterranean civilisation; the Phoenicians* HAD *the advantage of being in its midst.* In both these sentences, the verb of the first clause actually signals a time later than that of the second. The English language does not forbid this arrangement, although good style may more frequently dictate the opposite ordering, or the use of the Past Perfect (see §§ 73–4).

OTHER USES OF THE SIMPLE PAST

21   The Past Tense is used in dependent clauses (except in noun clauses of indirect speech) to express HYPOTHETICAL meaning:

It's time we *had* a holiday. | If you *loved* me, you wouldn't do such a thing.

Discussion of this use is postponed until §§ 163–8.

22   Two extensions of the normal past meaning have to be mentioned. First, the Past Tense, in that it deals with past events, is the natural form of the verb to employ in narrative, whether the events narrated are true historical events or the fictional events of a novel. There has grown up a convention of using the Past for narrative even when the events portrayed are supposed to take place in the future, as in science fiction:

In the year A.D. 2201, the interplanetary transit vehicle Zeno VII *made* a routine journey to the moon with thirty people on board.

We are invited, by this convention, to look at future events as if from a vantage-point even further in the future. Any narrative normally presupposes, in the imagination, such a retrospective view.

23   A second special development of the normal past meaning is the use of the Past Tense, in some contexts of everyday conversation, TO REFER TO THE PRESENT; in particular, to the present feelings or thoughts of the speaker or hearer:

> *A*: *Did* you *want* me?
> *B*:   Yes, I *hoped* you would give me a hand with the painting.

The subject of this exchange would probably be the *present* wishes of Speaker *B*, despite the use of the Past Tense. The Present and Past are, in fact, broadly interchangeable in this context; but there is quite an important difference of tone. The effect of the Past Tense is to make the request indirect, and therefore more polite. We may explain the polite connotation here as a hint that the speaker is no longer necessarily committed to the feelings mentioned; that he is quite prepared to change his own attitude in the light of that of the listener. The Present Tense (*I hope* . . .) in this situation would seem rather brusque and demanding – it would make the request difficult to refuse without impoliteness. The Past Tense, on the other hand, avoids a confrontation of wills. Politeness also extends to the original question *Did you want me?* The logically expected Present Tense (*Do you want me?*) might have peremptory overtones, and would seem to say: 'Oh, it's you, is it? You always want something'.

Other verbs similarly used are *wonder* and *think*:

> I *wondered* if you'd look after my dog while I go shopping. | I *thought* I might come and see you later this evening.

As before, the speaker is purportedly testing the listener's reaction to a past attitude to which he confesses, whilst pretending that his present attitude is undetermined.

a. In this context, the Progressive Past is frequently preferred, as it adds a further overtone of politeness to that of the Simple Past: *I was wondering* . . . etc. (see § 43a).

b. The indirect and polite connotation of the Past here might suggest that the origin of the usage lies in the hypothetical use of the Past, rather than in the 'past time' use. This is unlikely, however, since hypothetical meaning is expressed by the ordinary Past Tense only in dependent clauses. In main clauses, it is normally expressed by *would* + Infinitive (see § 166).

c. The above usage is comparable with the use of the Past to point a contrast with an unspoken present alternative: *I* THOUGHT *you were leaving* (*sc.* '. . . but now I see you're not'). In both cases the 'non-present' element of Past Tense meaning is emphasised, and the 'definite time' element is suppressed: there is nothing in such sentences to say precisely *when* the speaker had the attitude or opinion mentioned. (See § 64).

d. This polite usage may be more developed in BE than in AE.

SIMPLE PRESENT: IMAGINARY USES

24   Before closing the examination of Simple Present and Past Tenses, we must look at one or two less important uses of the Simple Present with reference not to real time, but to IMAGINARY PRESENT time.

25   Technically, a distinction may be made between the historic use of the present (illustrated in § 15), and its FICTIONAL use. It is customary for novelists and story writers to use the Past Tense to describe imaginary happenings (whether past, present or future with respect to real time), so that the employment of the Simple Present in fiction (except in direct speech) strikes one as a deviation from normal practice. Some writers use the Present in imitation of the popular historic present of spoken narrative. For more serious writing, transposition into the fictional present is a device of dramatic heightening; it puts the reader in the place of someone actually witnessing the events as they are described:

> Mr. Tulkinghorn *takes* out his papers, *asks* permission to place them on a golden talisman of a table at my Lady's elbow, *puts* on his spectacles, and *begins* to read by the light of a shaded lamp.
>
> (Dickens, *Bleak House*, Ch. 2)

As with the Simple Past, the succession of Simple Present forms so used tends to represent a sequence, rather than a coincidence, of events.

a. In some other narrative contexts, it is not the Past Tense, but the Present Tense that is conventional. For example, stage directions: *Mr. Mulberry enters hastily and bows to Lady Frolic.* Whatever the imagined time of the play's action, in the make-believe of the theatre anything that happens on the stage is 'in the present' as it comes before the audience's eyes. Also in the spirit of the stage-direction are narrative interpolations in and introductions to comic-strips.

b. Similarly, instalments of serial stories (whether on the radio, or on television, or in popular magazines) until recently used to begin with recapitulations of previous instalments in the Present Tense (The Story So Far: *John Cunningham* VISITS *his aunt, Mavis Bott, in her secluded Cornish home* . . .). Perhaps this convention, now often superseded by Past Tense summary, came from the habit, adopted by novelists such as Smollett and Dickens, of giving chapter summaries in the Present Tense in place of simple chapter titles: *Chapter XXI. Madame Mantalini* FINDS *Herself in a Situation of some Difficulty, and Miss Nickleby* FINDS *Herself in no Situation at all.* (*Nicholas Nickleby*)

26   Two special uses of the Present Tense hard to classify are (*a*) that of the travelogue itinerary:

> To reach Chugwell, we *make* our way up to the source of the River Ede, then *skirt* the bleak slopes of Windy Beacon, crowned by sparse remains of a Bronze Age fort.

and (*b*) that of the instruction booklet:

> You *test* an air-leak by disconnecting the delivery pipe at the carburettor and pumping petrol into a container.

The second of these has a spoken counterpart in such verbal directions as:

> You *take* the first turning on the left past the roundabout, then you *cross* a bridge and *bear* right until you reach the Public Library.

In each of these cases, it is possible to interpret the sequence of events iteratively; for instance, one might preface the set of street directions: *Every time you want to get to the library* . . . (understanding *you* as an impersonal pronoun equivalent to *one*). On the other hand, perhaps a more plausible interpretation is that of the 'imaginary present': the person describing the set of events envisages them as happening now, before his mind's eye, while he speaks.

a. Notice that there is a difference between the *you*+Present Tense construction illustrated above and the *you*+Imperative construction of *You leave this to me, You mind your own business, etc. You* preceding an Imperative receives sentence stress, whereas normally as subject of a finite verb it does not.

Two

Progressive Aspect

27 Progressive Aspect. PROGRESSIVE ASPECT REFERRING TO TEMPORARY HAPPENINGS: *28* temporariness; *29* duration; *30* limited duration; *31* not necessarily complete; *32* 'temporal frame' effect; *33* there is not always a 'temporal frame'. CLASSES OF VERB WITH THE PROGRESSIVE ASPECT: *34*; *35* A 'Momentary Verbs', *35* B 'Transitional Event Verbs'; *36* C 'Activity Verbs', *36* D 'Process Verbs'; *37* verbs normally incompatible with the Progressive; *37* E 'Verbs of Inert Perception', *37* F 'Verbs of Inert Cognition', *37* G 'State Verbs of Having and Being'; *38* H 'Verbs of Bodily Sensation'. APPARENT EXCEPTIONS *39*; *40–1* verbs in class E; *42–3* verbs in class F; *44–5* verbs in class G; *46* further exceptions. PROGRESSIVE ASPECT— OTHER USES *47*; *48–50* habitual or iterative use of Progressive; *51* future use; *52* 'persistent' or 'continuous' use.

27   The term PROGRESSIVE has frequently been used, and is used here, to designate those verb constructions in which the *-ing* form of the verb is preceded by a form of the verb *to be*: (*i*)*s working*, (*wi*)*ll be working*, (*ha*)*s been working*, etc. The term is selected not because of any positive virtue it has, but because it at least avoids the misleading semantic associations which belong to other terms commonly used by grammarians: 'durative', 'temporary', 'continuous', etc. This chapter complements Chapter I in that it contrasts the Progressive Present and Past Tenses with the Simple Present and Past. Consideration of other Progressive Tenses (Perfect, Future, etc.) will be left until later (see §§ 75–82, 105–8).

PROGRESSIVE ASPECT REFERRING TO TEMPORARY HAPPENINGS

28   First, let us consider the most important function of the Progressive Aspect, which is to refer to TEMPORARY situations, activities, or goings-on:

Where's Joan? She's cooking the dinner.
What on earth are you doing? I'm trying to play the violin.
What's happening? The river's overflowing its banks.

These examples illustrate the Progressive Present: the temporary situation includes the present moment in its time-span, stretching for a limited period into the past and into the future. To distinguish the Progressive Present so used from the Simple Present, it is necessary to stress three separate aspects of meaning:

1 The Progressive Form indicates *duration* (and is thus distinguished from the non-durative 'instantaneous present').

2 The Progressive Form indicates *limited duration* (and is thus distinguished from the 'unrestrictive present').

3 The Progressive Form indicates that the *happening need not be complete* (and is again thereby distinguished from the 'instantaneous present').

Points (1) and (2) show that the Progressive *stretches* the time span of an 'event verb', but *compresses* the time span of a 'state verb'. It must be emphasised again, however, that this is a matter of psychological rather than real time: it is possible for the same incident to be described by either the Simple or the Progressive Present, depending upon a speaker's point of view.

Let us now examine each of the three features of meaning separately.

29 The durative element of meaning is seen in the contrast of *I raise my arm!* or *The house falls down!* with *I am raising my arm* or *The house is falling down*. The first pair suggests a sudden movement, and second a more gradual one. With the Progressive Tense, the event is no longer instantaneous: it stretches into the past and into the future.

a. It has been noticed that whereas radio commentators for fast-moving sports (football, tennis, boxing, etc.) tend to use the Simple Present (*Greaves* SHOOTS *for goal* . . .; *Mrs. King* SERVES . . .; *Walker* DUCKS . . .), those describing more 'leisurely' sports (cricket, rowing, golf) rely more upon the Progressive Present: *Trueman* IS RUNNING *up to bowl*; *Oxford* ARE ROWING *well* . . .; This is not surprising, since in such sports it is more difficult to see the stages of the match or contest as having no duration.

30 The difference between unlimited and LIMITED DURATION is evident from the following sentences, in which the Simple Present, in its unrestrictive use, contrasts with the Progressive Present:

My watch *works* perfectly (permanent state – 'my watch is generally a reliable one'). | My watch *is working* perfectly (temporary state – could mean 'my watch is not particularly reliable; it has gone wrong in the past, and may do so again').

I *live* in Wimbledon (permanent residence). | I *am living* in Wimbledon (temporary residence).

I *enjoy* the seaside ('I like holidays by the sea in general'). | I *am enjoying* the seaside ('I am enjoying this particular holiday').

a. Along with the 'temporary' meaning of the Progressive there often goes a notion that the state is 'actual' and 'particular'. *I am enjoying the seaside* would be spoken when the speaker is actually at the seaside; this is not necessarily true of *I enjoy the seaside*. One may observe a similar difference between *This basin is leaking* (actual: even now water is escaping) and *This basin leaks* (potential: this is a permanent quality of the basin); similarly *These shirts wash easily* and *These shirts are washing easily*.

31   That the action expressed by the Progressive Present is NOT NECESSARILY COMPLETE is best illustrated by 'event verbs' which signal a transition from one state to another (e.g. *become, die, fall, get, go, stop*). Using the instantaneous present, one might exclaim *The bus stops!*, so indicating the vehicle's arrival at a state of rest. But *The bus is stopping* means only that the bus is slowing down towards a stop: cessation of movement is not guaranteed.

This part of the Progressive meaning is more noticeable in the Past Tense:

The man *was drowning*. | The man *drowned*.

To the first sentence one could add . . . *but I jumped into the water and saved him*; but not to the second, which implies that the man actually died.

The following sentences illustrate lack of certainty about completeness in another context:

I *was reading* from 10 p.m. to 11 p.m. | I *read* from 10 to 11 p.m.

The Simple Past tells us that the speaker started to read at 10 o'clock and finished at 11 o'clock. The Progressive, however, does not specify either the time of beginning or the time of completing the activity: all we know is that reading was in progress for that hour. Hence it would be a fitting answer from a suspect being interrogated by a detective. The detective would ask *What* WERE *you* DOING *between*

10 p.m. and 11 p.m.? being uninterested in whether the activity persisted after that period or not; and the suspect would reply in kind.

Notice a further difference between *I was reading a book that evening* and *I read a book that evening*. The Simple Past here suggests that the speaker reached the end of his book before the end of the evening; completion in this sense is not implied by *was reading*.

32   The Progressive Aspect generally has the effect of surrounding a particular event or moment by a 'temporal frame', which can be diagrammed simply: ⟨‿‿‿‿ . ‿‿‿⟩. That is, within the flow of time, there is some point of reference from which the temporary eventuality indicated by the verb can be seen as stretching into the future and into the past. With the Progressive Present, the point of orientation is normally identical with 'now', the present moment of real time. But in the Progressive Past, some other definite point of reference must be assumed. Often this point is made explicit by an adverbial phrase or clause:

> *This time last year* I was travelling round the world. | *Five minutes later* the rescue party was leaving. | He was looking very ill *when I last saw him.*

In both Past and Present Tense narrative, the Progressive often forms a 'temporal frame' around an action denoted by a non-progressive form; in this case, whereas the relationship of meaning between two neighbouring Simple Past forms is usually one of *time-sequence*, the relationship between a Progressive and a Simple Past form is one of *time-inclusion*. The contrast can be studied in these two sentences:

> When we *arrived* she *made* some fresh coffee.
> When we *arrived* she *was making* some fresh coffee.

The first example tells us that the coffee-making *followed* the arrival; the second, that the arrival took place *during* the coffee-making.

a. A Simple Tense verb in a main clause is often 'framed' in this manner by a Progressive Tense verb in a subordinate noun clause: *I asked him what he was thinking about* (i.e. 'at the time when I asked him').

33   The 'temporal frame' effect is not an independent feature of the Progressive form's meaning; it follows, rather, from the notion of 'limited duration'. Whenever a point of time or an event is in a contemporaneous relation with a happening of duration, it is natural that the durational happening should overlap the durationless event or point in both directions–in short, that a 'temporal frame' should be set up.

When no event or point of time is in question, however, the framing effect does not occur. For example:

They *were watching* a football match on Saturday afternoon.

Here a temporary occupation is related to a period. There is no point round which the 'watching' forms a frame: we would be more inclined to say, in fact, that the afternoon forms a 'temporal frame' round the 'watching', since we know that normally football matches begin and end within the duration of an afternoon.

Another case where there is no 'frame' is that where two Progressive Past verbs are put next to one another:

While she *was working* hard in the kitchen, her husband *was sitting* down in front of the television set.

All we know here is that the two activities were *at some time or other* simultaneous. We know nothing about the relation between their starting-points or finishing-points: whether the wife began working in the kitchen before her husband began watching television is an irrelevance. The four main possibilities may therefore be diagrammed thus (where a='working in the kitchen', and b='watching television'):

The framing effect is, incidentally, rarely found with the Perfect Progressive Tenses (see §§ 75–81).

CLASSES OF VERB WITH THE PROGRESSIVE ASPECT

34   The Progressive Aspect varies its effect according to the type of meaning conveyed by the verb. We have already noted this with 'event verbs' and 'state verbs'; but now it is convenient to distinguish further classes of verb (or more correctly, of verbal meaning).

35   We begin with two classes of 'event verb'.

A.   'MOMENTARY VERBS' (*hiccough, hit, jump, kick, knock, nod, tap, wink*, etc.). These verbs refer to happenings so momentary that it is difficult to think of them as having duration. Consequently, the Progressive form, in attributing duration to them, forces one to think of a series of events, rather than of a single event. Compare *He nodded* (a single movement) with *He was nodding* (a repeated movement); *He jumped up and down* with *He was jumping up and down; Someone fired a gun at me* with *Someone was firing a gun at me.*

B. 'TRANSITIONAL EVENT VERBS' (*arrive, die, fall, land, leave, lose, stop,* etc.). As exemplified earlier with *The bus is stopping* (§ 31), 'event verbs' denoting transition into a state are used with the Progressive to indicate an *approach* to the transition, rather than the transition itself:

> The train was arriving. | The helicopter was landing. | The old man was dying.

We could even argue that a different meaning of the verb comes into play in the switch from Simple Past to Progressive Past: *die* in *He was dying* indicates a process which ends in death; *die* in *He died* pin-points the actual moment of transition, the completion of the process.

36 Next, here are two classes of verb typically accompanying the Progressive form.

C. 'ACTIVITY VERBS' (*drink, eat, play, rain, read, work, write,* etc.). Although these verbs can be used with the Simple Tenses in an 'event' sense, they more usually occur with the Progressive, as they refer to a continuing, though bounded, activity:

> What *are* you *doing?* | I'*m writing* a letter. | They'*re* still *eating* their dinner.

'Activity' is not altogether a satisfactory term for this class: not all the verbs included refer to human occupations. The important point is that the verb tells us something is 'going on'.

D. 'PROCESS VERBS' (*change, grow, mature, slow down, widen, deteriorate,* etc.). As a process ordinarily has duration, but not indefinite duration, these verbs also tend to go with the Progressive Aspect: *The weather* IS CHANGING *for the better; They*'RE WIDENING *the road;* etc.

37 Most difficulties over the use of the Progressive Aspect arise with classes of verbs which are NORMALLY INCOMPATIBLE WITH THE PRO-

GRESSIVE. The most important of these verbs is the verb *to be*: it is possible to say *He is ill* (unrestrictive present) but not normally *★He is being ill*, even though the illness referred to in this sentence is presumably a temporary rather than permanent indisposition. Verbs not combining with the Progressive can be placed in certain rough semantic categories. Meaning, unfortunately, is not the sole determining factor, since virtually synonymous sentences can be found, one in which the Progressive is allowable, and one in which it is not:

He *is suffering* from influenza= He *is* ill with influenza.

It seems as if usage in this area is to some extent erratic and dependent purely upon choice of vocabulary.

A further difficulty is that many of the verbs so classified can occur with the Progressive Aspect in special contexts. Such exceptional uses can usually be explained by postulating the verb's membership (perhaps through a special transfer of meaning) of more than one verbal category. First, however, let us consider the straight-forward cases of verbs inimical to the Progressive Aspect.

E.   'VERBS OF INERT PERCEPTION' (*feel, hear, see, smell, taste* – see §§ 40–1 for exceptions). The term 'inert' is used for these common verbs, to distinguish perception of the kind denoted by *see*, where the perceiver is merely passively receptive, from that of (say) *look at*, where the perceiver is actively directing his attention towards some object.

I *could feel/felt* something hard under my foot.
        (NOT *★I *was feeling* . . .)
I *could hear/heard* a knocking at the door.
        (NOT *★I *was hearing* . . .)
I *could see/saw* someone through the window.
        (NOT *★I *was seeing* . . .)
I *could smell/smelt* onions cooking.
        (NOT *★I *was smelling* . . .)
I *could taste/tasted* sugar in the tea.
        (NOT *★I *was tasting* . . .)

a. The difference between the variant constructions with and without *could* is that the *could* form denotes a state, whereas the Simple Past form denotes an event. Thus *I could hear a door slamming* indicates a continuing and repeated noise; *I heard a door slam*, a single momentary percussion.(*★I could hear a door slam* seems odd because of the clash of duration in *could hear* with momentariness in *slam*.) There is a parallel contrast in the Present

Tense: *I see a bird*! is a case of the instantaneous use of the Present, and means much the same as *I catch sight of a bird*! Here, as elsewhere, the instantaneous use is rather unusual and melodramatic. The more natural *can* construction (*I can see a bird*) stands in place of the unrestrictive use of the Present.

F.   'VERBS OF INERT COGNITION' (*believe, forget, hope, imagine, know, suppose, understand*, etc. − see §§ 42–3 for exceptions), like the verbs of perception above, are passive in meaning. The Simple Present in this case refers to a mental state, and so belongs to the category 'unrestrictive present', even though a limitation on the duration of the state may be implied:

> I *think* that they are coming.
> > (RATHER THAN: *I *am thinking* that . . .)
> I *believe* we have met already.
> > (RATHER THAN: *I *am believing* we have . . .)

Similarly:

> I *forget* what I paid for the house. | He *imagines* everything to be easy. | We *understand* your difficulty.

As the examples suggest, verbs with this type of meaning are frequently followed by a noun clause. Attitudinal verbs such as *like, hate,* and *prefer* may be placed under the same heading.

a. *Feel* can be a 'verb of cognition' (Class F) as well as a 'verb of perception' (Class E): *I* FEEL (i.e. it is my feeling or opinion) *that some action must be taken immediately.*

b. Verbs such as *read, tell,* and *find* referring to the result of communication (see § 16) may also be placed in this class. For example, *John tells me . . .* means 'I *understand* as a result of John's having told me . . .'. *See* and *hear,* in addition to being 'verbs of perception', can be used in this cognitive sense: *I* SEE *you are having a house built*; *I* HEAR *the Wilberforces have fallen out with the Smiths* (not *I am seeing . . .* etc.).

c. It is significant that *know* is characteristically followed by the Progressive in sentences like *John* KNOWS *he* IS TALKING *nonsense*; *I like a man who* KNOWS *what he's* DOING. The state of knowledge and the activities of 'talking' and 'doing' are here concurrent; the time-spans are comparable, and therefore, but for the inclusion of *know* in Class F, we would expect matching verbal constructions − the Progressive Present in both cases.

G.   'STATE VERBS OF HAVING AND BEING' (*be, belong to, contain, consist of, cost, depend on, deserve, have, matter, own, resemble*, etc. − see § 44 for exceptions). In this class, together with the key verbs *be* and *have*, belong verbs which include, as part of their meaning, the notion of 'being' or 'having'. Often a paraphrase with *be* or *have* is possible: *matter=be important*; *own=have in one's possession*; *resemble=be like*; etc. (Incidentally, some verbs of Class F can also be so rendered: *I think=My opinion is . . .*; *I believe=My belief is . . .*; etc.).

> This carpet *belongs* to me. (NOT *This carpet *is belonging* to me.)
> I *own* this carpet. (NOT *I *am owning* this carpet.)
> Your age *doesn't matter*. (NOT *Your age *isn't mattering*.)

Similarly:

> This bread *contains* too much yeast. | Apples *cost* a lot at this time of year. | Whether the play is a success *depends* on you, the audience.

a. The use of *have* under consideration here is the 'state' *have* of *She has several sisters*; *I have a bad backache*, etc. (This *have* can be replaced by *have got* in BE.) There is also an 'activity' *have* which occurs freely with the Progressive Aspect, and which answers the question *What are you doing?*: *I am having breakfast/a party/a cigarette/a bath*, etc.

38   Finally, mention must be made of a small class of verbs which, when referring to a temporary state, can occur either with or without the Progressive:

H.   'VERBS OF BODILY SENSATION' (*ache, feel, hurt, itch, tingle,* etc.). There is apparently a free choice, without change of meaning, between *I feel hungry* and *I am feeling hungry*; between *My knee hurts* and *My knee is hurting*; etc. A difference should be noted between this meaning of *feel*, which is a question of *internal* sensation, and the meaning of *feel* as a 'verb of perception' (Class E above), denoting *external* sensation: *I can feel a stone in my shoe*, etc.

APPARENT EXCEPTIONS

39   There are many apparent exceptions to the rule that verbs of classes E, F, and G do not go with the Progressive Aspect. In general, however, these exceptions can be explained by postulating 'multiple class membership' of the verbs concerned. Such multiple membership has already been observed with the verb *feel*, which with different meanings belongs to classes E, F, and H.

40   VERBS IN CLASS E. *Feel*, *taste*, and *smell* can be used to indicate not only 'inert perception', but also 'active perception'. In the second case, they belong to the 'activity' category (Class C) and so may freely take the Progressive form:

INERT	ACTIVE
I *(can) smell* the perfume.	I*'m smelling* the perfume.
I *(can) feel* the ground.	I*'m feeling* the ground with my foot.
I *(can) taste* salt in my porridge.	I*'m tasting* the porridge, to see if it contains enough salt.

In the first sentence of each pair, the sensation simply 'happens' to me; but in the second, I go out of my way to focus my attention on some object. The second sentence answers the question *What are you doing?* and, as the examples show, may be supplemented by an adverbial expression of instrument or purpose.

However, the remaining two verbs in Class E, *see* and *hear*, are not used in the active sense, because the separate verbs *look at* and *listen to* are available for that function:

INERT	ACTIVE
I *(can) see* a bus in the distance.	I*'m looking at* a bus in the distance.
I *(can) hear* what he is saying.	I*'m listening* to what he is saying.

'Inert perception' is a more appropriate term than 'passive perception', since it is merely the absence of agency that is signified by the verb in the left-hand column. Likewise, perhaps 'agentive verb' or 'doing verb' would be a more suitable term for the type represented by *look at* and *listen to*; these verbs are not merely 'activity verbs' in the wide sense of Class C, but in the more precise sense of 'involving animate agency'.

a. A third class of perception verbs may more fittingly be called 'passive'; it consists of those verbs for which the grammatical subject is the object of perception: *That* SOUNDS *like Martha's voice*; *You* LOOK *tired*. Here again, although *see* and *hear* are matched by separate verbs (*look* and *sound*), the three verbs *smell*, *taste*, and *feel* do duty for the extra function: *This peach feels/smells/tastes good.* As the type of perception expressed is 'inert' rather than 'active', the Progressive is generally excluded: *★That is sounding like Martha's voice* is incorrect. Strangely, *look* is an exception to the rule: it is possible to say both *You look well* and *You're looking well*, perhaps because of an analogy with *I feel/am feeling well* (see Class H, § 38).

C

41   Before leaving Class E, we have to reckon with an acceptable use of the Progressive with *hear* in sentences like *I am hearing you clearly* (spoken, say, by a radio or telephone operator). The meaning here is 'I am receiving your message', and the effect of the Progressive is to place emphasis on the *process* of communication. We may argue, therefore, that in this context *hear* is interpreted as a 'process verb' (Class D).

42   Verbs in Class F are also occasionally found with the Progressive form:

> I'*m thinking* about what you said. | Surely you'*re imagining* things. | I'*m supposing*, for the purposes of this argument, that your intentions are unknown.

In the first of these examples, 'thinking' is felt to be a kind of work or mental exertion, equivalent to 'considering' or 'ruminating'. In the second, *imagining things* means 'entertaining or indulging yourself with illusions'. In the third, *I'm supposing that* . . . means 'I am making the temporary assumption that . . .' Each sentence, that is, suggests some positive mental activity. Therefore we may claim that in sentences of this kind, verbs normally of Class F are functioning, unusually, as 'activity verbs'.

43   The explanation above in § 42 does not meet cases of a special polite use of the Progressive with certain verbs of Class F:

> I'*m hoping* you'll give us some advice. | What *were* you *wanting?* | You *are forgetting* the moral arguments. | We'*re wondering* if you have any suggestions.

In idiomatic colloquial speech, this apparently unaccountable usage is often preferred to the regular Simple Present form *I hope . . . You forget* etc. The reason for this preference seems to be that the Progressive is a more tentative, and hence more polite method of expressing a mental attitude. There is, as we have seen (§ 28), a notion of 'temporariness' and 'possible incompleteness' about the Progressive form, and in the present context, it is extended to 'lack of commitment'. *I hope you'll give us some advice* leaves the addressee little room for polite refusal; but *I am hoping* implies that the speaker has not finally committed himself to the hope: he is ready to change his mind about his feelings should the listener's reaction be discouraging.

a. The Progressive therefore fulfills in this case a similar function to that of the Past Tense described in § 23: *I wondered if you'd give us some advice.* Indeed, the two forms may be combined in a Past Progressive construction with doubly self-deprecatory connotations: *I was wondering if you'd give us some advice*; *I was hoping you would look after the children for us.* The form of verb, for politeness, must be matched against the size of favour requested. The Past Progressive (most tentative) is appropriate to a request which will put the listener to considerable risk or inconvenience; the Simple Present (most direct) may be used politely only when the listener is invited to do something which is to his own advantage: *I hope you'll come and have dinner with us when you're in London next.*

44 VERBS IN CLASS G ('state verbs of having and being') may, like those of Classes E and F, combine with the Progressive Aspect where an 'activity' meaning may be supplied. The verb *to be* itself furnishes many examples. While it is virtually impossible to make sense of *★He is being tall* or *★The trees are being green*, there is no difficulty with *She is being kind*, because we are able to understand 'kindness' here as a mode of outward behaviour over which the person has control, rather than as an inherent trait of character. *She is being kind* means 'She is acting kindly towards someone', whereas *She is kind* means 'She is constitutionally good-natured'. Similar differences of meaning are seen in:

He's a fool (*i.e.* 'He can't help it – it's his nature').
He's being a fool (*i.e.* 'He's acting foolishly').

He's awkward (*i.e.* 'He's clumsy, gauche').
He's being awkward (*i.e.* 'He's being deliberately obstructive').

The car is difficult to drive (*i.e.* 'It's made that way').
The car is being difficult (*i.e.* 'It's going out of its way to cause trouble' – the car here is almost personified).

The Progressive is also permissible in *He's being good/useful/helpful/a nuisance/an angel.* Even if no recognised 'activity' meaning is available, one may frequently make sense of a sentence *X is being Y*, however improbable the context, by reading into it the idea of acting a part. *Today, my uncle is being Napoleon* could be said of an actor or a megalomaniac. *He is being sorry/afraid/happy* etc. could conceivably mean 'He is pretending to be sorry/afraid/happy'. A parallel though less likely example with the verb *have* is *My wife is having a headache* meaning 'My wife is pretending to have a headache'. (On the other hand, no element of showmanship is necessarily present in *My wife is having hysterics/a fit/a baby*–these are normal instances of the 'activity' or 'process' use of *have*.)

a. In a more precise analysis, it should be made clear that the contrast between *He is awkward* and *He is being awkward* is more complicated than suggested above. Whereas the Progressive Present here restricts the adjective to the meaning 'obstructionist', the Simple Present is ambiguous, allowing both 'state' and 'activity' interpretations. Two separate conditions of meaning are involved: (1) the time-span is temporary rather than permanent; and (2) the verb may be construed as referring to an activity with human agency. The first of these conditions is fulfilled in *He is hungry*, and the second in *He is awkward* (meaning 'He habitually goes out of his way to be obstructive'). Only when both conditions are present together, as in *He is being awkward*, does one expect the Progressive Aspect with the verb *to be*.

b. The encroachment of the 'state present' of *to be* on the 'limited duration present' normally expressed by the Progressive is clear from the synonymy of the following:

    The child is asleep=The child is sleeping.
    The train is in motion=The train is moving.
    The train is stationary=The train is standing still.

In each case, a sentence containing the Simple Present form *is* is matched in meaning with a sentence (on the right) containing the Present Progressive form of some other verb.

45   Certain other verbs of Class G can take the Progressive when accompanied by an expression like *more and more*:

    He *is resembling* his father more and more as the years go by. | The income of one's parents *is mattering* less in education these days. | Good food *is costing* more since devaluation.

The meaning of all these sentences (which are felt to be rather unnatural by some speakers) could be vaguely formulated 'This is the way things are going', and the explanation of the Progressive here seems to be that the verbs are no longer 'state verbs', but have been transferred to the class of 'process verbs'. *Resemble*, for example, here means 'to become like' rather than 'to be like'.

46   Unavoidably, there are some exceptions to the rule which have . not been dealt with here. Some instances that one may hear in colloquial English to-day seem difficult to fit into any system of rules and classes. It has to be accepted that this is an area of usage which is unstable at the present time, and is probably undergoing continuing change.

a. For instance, it is difficult to find an explanation for one common application of the Past Progressive in familiar colloquial speech:

I *was* recently *reading* about an invention which may turn garbage into soil. | Albert *was saying* that coal prices are going up.

The Progressive Past refers here to fairly recent communicative happenings (*the other day* is a common adverbial collocation). There is no feeling of a 'temporal frame' round a past moment of time; nor does there appear to be any suggestion of the tentativeness of *I was wondering* or *I was hoping* (see § 43*a*). The only part of the Progressive meaning relevant is 'lack of completeness'. In answer to a question *Did you hear about that awful Mrs. Betts quarrelling with her neighbour?*, one might reply *Yes, my daughter Liz* WAS TELLING *me about it.* This would not imply total knowledge, and so would politely leave the way open for a continuation of the story. But the tale-bearer might be silenced by a similar reply with the Simple Past Tense (*Yes, Liz* TOLD *me about it*), as this would carry the presupposition 'Yes, I know the whole story, so don't bother to tell me'. One peculiarity of this usage is that the Past Tense does not suggest a specific earlier point of time reference. One could say *Yes, the wife was telling me about it* without mentioning or implying some definite point of time at which the telling happened. Another point is that the Progressive Past cannot be used in this way in questions; one would never hear ★*Were you hearing about that awful Mrs. Betts . . .?*

PROGRESSIVE ASPECT: OTHER USES

47   Apart from the major use of the Progressive Aspect to refer to single temporary happenings, there are four other less important uses to be considered.

48   First, there are two separate HABITUAL or ITERATIVE uses of the Progressive, corresponding to the single habitual use of Simple Past and Present illustrated in §§ 13 and 19.

49   Consider the following sentences:

I'*m taking* dancing lessons this winter. | In those days, we *were getting* up at 7 o'clock. | Mr. Robinson *is cycling* to work until his car is repaired.

In these cases, the Progressive concept of 'limited duration' is applied not to the individual events that make up the series, but to the series as a whole. The meaning is 'HABIT IN EXISTENCE OVER A LIMITED PERIOD'—the period in question being generally specified by an adverbial expression, as in the examples above. On the other hand, there may be no adverbial, as in *I'M TAKING dancing lessons*. It is the temporariness of the habit that is important: *I'M TAKING dancing lessons* suggests a shorter period than *I TAKE dancing lessons*.

The iterative element of meaning may well be made clear by an adverbial expression of frequency: *The trains are arriving late PRACTICALLY EVERY DAY this winter*.

a. Adverbs of indefinite frequency may not be so used, however: *⋆I am SOMETIMES walking to work until my car is repaired*.

50   The second habitual meaning is REPETITION OF EVENTS OF LIMITED DURATION:

> Whenever I visit him he *is mowing* his lawn. | Don't call on them at 7.30—they're usually *having* dinner. | By sunrise the labourers *were* normally *making* their way to work.

Here the notion of limited duration is applied not to the habit as a whole, but to the individual events of which the habit is composed. The result of substituting the Progressive for the Simple Present is thus to *stretch* the time-span of the event: compare the first sentence above with *Whenever I visit him he MOWS his lawn*. Normally, this meaning of the Progressive is accompanied by adverbial modification naming a point of time against which the temporary activity is seen as a 'frame'. When no adverbial of time is present, there must nevertheless be a point of time implied by the context. Thus to the second example above we could add the words . . . *at that time* (viz. 7.30), making explicit what is otherwise implicit.

An adverbial phrase of frequency may also be added: OFTEN *when I pass she is sitting there on the doorstep, watching the world go by*. With the past tense, absence of frequency modification leads to ambiguity as to habitual or non-habitual meaning. This is evident in the third example above, which, if *normally* is omitted, may refer either to a single act of going to work, or to an event regularly repeated on each work day.

a. The point of reference 'framed' by the Progressive Tense in this iterative sense is often indicated by a verb introducing a noun clause within which the Progressive form occurs: *He rarely LETS us know what he IS DOING; You never LISTEN to what people ARE SAYING*.

51   The Progressive Present may, like the Simple Present, refer to anticipated happenings in the future:

> Denis *is buying* me a new coat for my birthday. | We*'re visiting* Aunt Rose tomorrow. | I hear you*'re moving* to a new job.

Also happenings anticipated in the past may be expressed by the Progressive Past Tense: *As we* WERE VISITING *them the next day, there was no point in sending the parcel by post.* More will be said of this future or anticipatory use in §§ 97–100.

52   Finally, there is a special idiomatic meaning of the Progressive, marked by the absence of the 'temporary' element of the normal Progressive meaning:

> Day by day we *are getting* nearer to death.

The sense here is one of PERSISTENT or CONTINUOUS activity; it is as if, in the 'process' use of the Progressive, the durational element of meaning overrides in this instance the temporary element. The uninterrupted nature of the activity is usually underlined by the presence of adverbs or adverbial phrases such as *continually, constantly, for ever,* and *always*:

> My father was *for ever* getting into trouble with the law. | I'm *continually* forgetting people's names. | I know a man who's *always* giving his wife expensive presents.

Notice that *always* in this context is a synonym for *continually*; it does not mean what *always* means in the corresponding Simple Present construction: *I know a man who always* GIVES *his wife expensive presents.* The sense of this last sentence is 'I know a man who gives his wife an expensive present on every occasion' (*i.e.* on every occasion when husbands normally give wives presents); but with the Progressive, the rough sense is 'There is never a time at which this man is not giving his wife expensive presents'.

Obviously there is an element of colloquial hyperbole or exaggeration in such sentences. Further, their tone is often one of irritation or amused disparagement. Anyone who used a sentence about *a man who is always giving people lifts* would tend to have a critical attitude towards the man, even though his habit of giving lifts might generally be considered laudable by other people.

Three

The Expression of Past Time

53   It is well known that English has two chief ways of indicating past time by means of the verb: the Past Tense (*I worked, he wrote,* etc.) and the Perfect Aspect (*I have worked, he has written,* etc.); also that these two can be combined to form the Past Perfect (or 'Pluperfect') (*I had worked, he had written,* etc.) signifying 'past in the past'. My main task, in this chapter, is to show how the Perfect is distinguished in meaning from the Past, first of all concentrating on the Present Perfect Tense.

At its most general, the Perfect Aspect is used for a past happening which is seen in relation to a later event or time. Thus the present perfect means 'past-time-related-to-present-time'.

PRESENT PERFECT TENSE

54   The Present Perfect, as distinct from the Simple Past Tense, is often described as referring to 'past with present relevance', or 'past involving the present'. There is a great deal of truth in this description, but on its own it is too vague to tell us exactly when and when not to use the Present Perfect. There are two distinct ways in which a past event may be related to the present by means of the Perfect: (a) it may involve a TIME PERIOD lasting up to the Present, and (b) it may have RESULTS persisting at the present time. Moreover, there are not just two, but four different senses of the Present Perfect, one of them occurring with 'state verbs' and three with 'event verbs'. We begin with the former.

55 STATE-UP-TO-THE-PRESENT. With 'state verbs', present involvement means that the state extends over a period lasting up to the present moment:

> We've *lived* in London since last September (*i.e.* 'London is where we are living now'). | *Have* you *known* the Faulkners for long? | That house *has been* empty for ages.

The *period* mentioned extends up to the present moment, but since 'state verbs' are of undefined time-span, the *state itself* may extend into the future: e.g. *We've lived here all our lives, and mean to live here for many years to come.*

The Past Tense would be unacceptable in BE in the first of the three examples above (being incompatible with the preposition *since*), and in the other two examples would mean that the period is already complete and in the past: *That house was empty for ages* ('. . . but now it's been sold and occupied'). (In AE *We lived* and *We've lived* could be interchangeable in the first sentence.)

This 'state' use of the Present Perfect is almost compulsorily accompanied by an adverbial of duration: the absence of an adverbial (e.g. *We have lived in London*) usually indicates not a state at all, but an event in the indefinite past (see § 56 below). There are exceptions, however, where a period leading up to the present, although not actually mentioned, is implied by context or the meaning of the clause. In *He's lived a good life*, duration up to the present is understood, because there is an implicit period 'during his life'; in *You've outstayed your welcome*, the word *outstay* in like manner incorporates the durational meaning 'for too long'.

a. Further exception must be made for verbs used in one of the 'non-progressive' categories (see §§ 37-8). With these verbs, the Simple Present Perfect also does service for a period of 'limited duration' normally expressed by the Present Perfect Progressive, for which the requirement of an accompanying adverbial does not apply. In answer to *Why haven't you been writing to me?* one might reply *I've been too angry to write*, or *I've been ill*. Here the verb *to be* (of Class G) describes a temporary situation, for which the Progressive form would elsewhere be appropriate.

56   INDEFINITE PAST. With 'event verbs', the Present Perfect may refer to some indefinite happening in the past:

> *Have* you *been* to America? | He's a man who *has experienced* suffering. | I*'ve known* them to strike their children in front of visitors. | All my family *have had* measles.

Often the indefinite meaning is reinforced adverbially, especially by *ever*, *never*, or *before* (*now*).

By 'indefiniteness' here are meant two things: first, the number of events is unspecified – it may be one or more than one; secondly, the time is also left unspecified. Therefore to put it more carefully, the meaning of the Present Perfect here is 'at-least-once-before-now'. The number of events, it is true, can be mentioned adverbially: *I've been to America three times*; but if there is an adverbial of time-when to specify the exact time, the Present Perfect becomes inappropriate, and must be replaced by the Simple Past: not *★I've BEEN to America last year*, but *I* WENT *to America last year*.

a. The indefinite past meaning of the Perfect, like the state-up-to-the-present meaning, does not often occur without adverbial reinforcement. On the rare occasions when it does so occur, the verb *have* tends to be stressed, and the whole clause to imply some kind of reservation: I *have eaten* lobster (with a fall of intonation on *have* and a rise on *lobster*) ('. . . but I can't say I enjoyed it'). Or I *have played* tennis ('. . . but not very often').

57   At first glance, it looks as if there is no element of 'present involvement' in this use of the Present Perfect, any more than there is in the Simple Past. But in fact, a more precise definition of the indefinite past use must indicate that a period of time leading up to the present is involved here, just as in the state use of the Present Perfect. Once again, the 'indefinite past' definition must be revised, and more exactly formulated as: 'at-least-once-in-a-period-leading-up-to-the-present'. This longer wording, when applied to the preceding examples, adds nothing material to the more concise label 'indefinite past'. But consider these other examples:

Have you visited the Gauguin exhibition? (i.e. 'while it has been on'). | The dustman hasn't called at our house (i.e. 'to-day').

The first of these sentences implies that the Gauguin exhibition is still running, whereas the Simple Past (*Did you visit . . .?*) would have made it clear that the exhibition is over. In the same way, the second sentence is spoken with a special time period (probably a day) in mind: it does not mean that the dustman has not called at least once in the past; it means rather that the dustman has not called during a period in which his regular visit is expected. There is a general tendency of self-centredness in human speech, whereby, unless otherwise specified, we understand a word or phrase to refer to something close at hand rather than distant. It is this principle that is at work in these sentences; and if we recognise that the indefinite past meaning always involves a period leading up to the present, it is easy to see how this period can become reduced, by subjective assumption, from 'always' to 'within the last few days', or even 'within the last few minutes'. In other sentences, the restricted period is made explicit: *Have you heard from the Joneses* SINCE CHRISTMAS?

The assumption of proximity is noticed in a less determinate way in utterances like *Have you seen my slippers?* or *The electrician has been* (BE, = ' . . . has visited our house'). If the adverbs *recently* and *just* are respectively added to these sentences, there is scarcely no change of meaning, as this simply makes the 'nearness' of the event explicit.

The sense of 'nearness' is quite common, so that it is worth recognising a sub-category of the indefinite past meaning, that of the RECENT INDEFINITE PAST. This is partly separated from the more general indefinite past meaning by its association with the adverbs *just, already, recently*, and *yet*. *Always, never, ever*, and *before*, on the other hand, single out the more general meaning. Compare, for instance, *Have you* EVER *been to America?* with *Has the dustman called* YET?

a. In AE, the recent indefinite past is more frequently expressed by the Simple Past Tense (which would be unnatural for a British speaker in this context) than by the Present Perfect.

58 HABIT-IN-A-PERIOD-LEADING-UP-TO-THE-PRESENT. The habitual or iterative use of the Present Perfect with 'event verbs' is illustrated by:

Mr. Phillips *has sung* in this choir for fifty years. | I've always *walked* to work. | The news *has been broadcast* at ten o'clock for as long as I can remember.

Since a habit (as that term has been understood here) is a state consisting of repeated events, this use closely resembles the 'state' use of the Present Perfect described in § 55 above. As was observed there, the habit or state may continue through the present moment into the future, and an adverbial of duration is usually required: *Mr. Phillips has sung in this choir* without the adverbial phrase becomes an example of the indefinite past meaning. Often, the habit element is emphasised by an adverbial of frequency: *The machine has been serviced* EVERY MONTH *since we bought it.*

59   RESULTATIVE PAST. The Present Perfect is also used in reference to a past event to imply that the result of that event is still operative at the present time. This meaning is clearest with 'transitional event verbs' (§ 35) denoting the switch from one state to another. The final (and present) state implied by the Perfect is indicated in brackets in these typical examples:

The taxi *has arrived* (i.e. 'The taxi is now here').
He *has been given* a camera ('He now has the camera').
I've *recovered* from my illness ('I'm now well again').
Someone *has broken* her doll ('The doll is now broken').

In other examples, the resultative inference is still there, even though it is not quite so obvious from the verb's meaning:

I've *had/taken* a bath ('I'm now clean').
He's *cut* his hand with a knife ('The cut is still there, *i.e.* has not yet healed').

The resultative meaning needs no support from adverbials. It is sometimes indistinguishable (or at least difficult to distinguish) from the recent indefinite past use (§ 57). One may argue, for instance, that the question *Have you seen my slippers?* is really a question about the present consequences of seeing the slippers; i.e. 'Do you know where they are?'.

a. Compare a similar resultative use of past participles: *a broken doll, a painted ceiling, an injured arm.* These examples contrast with past participles of 'state verbs', where the meaning is 'unrestrictive present': *an honoured colleague*; *a known gambler*; *a feared opponent*. These cannot be paraphrased by a clause with a Present Perfect verb form: *a feared opponent* means that the opponent *is* feared, not that he *has been* feared.

b. There are two Perfect forms of the verb *go*: *have + been* and *have + gone*. The difference in meaning between them is that the first is indefinite or habitual, whereas the second is resultative, indicating transition into a present state of absence. *He has gone to America* implies he is still there; *He has been to America*, that he has since returned.

c. As the notions of completeness and result are clearly connected, it seems appropriate to note at this point the completive emphasis of the Present Perfect in some rather oracular utterances in elevated style: *What I have written, I have written*. Here the effect of the Perfect is 'What I have written must stay there—it cannot be altered or added to'.

PRESENT PERFECT AND SIMPLE PAST

60   Having noted the four principal meanings of the Present Perfect, let us now review the contrasts and points of overlap between these meanings and that of the Simple Past. As a means of referring to the past, the Present Perfect differs from the Simple Past on three counts, viz. continuation up to the present, present result, and indefinite time.

61   CONTINUATION UP TO THE PRESENT TIME. This element of meaning is found in the state-up-to-the-present, in the habit-up-the-present and (to a degree) in the indefinite past meaning. The contrast of the 'state' Perfect with the Past is evident in:

His sister *has been* an invalid all her life (*i.e.* 'She is still alive').

His sister *was* an invalid all her life (*i.e.* 'She is now dead').

The same contrast is made with the habitual use in:

For generations, Nepal *has produced* the world's greatest soldiers. ('The nation of Nepal still exists').

For generations, Sparta *produced* Greece's greatest warriors. (This permits, but does not compel, us to infer that 'The state of Sparta no longer exists'.)

Again, here is the same point illustrated with the indefinite past use:

Has Samuel Beckett *written* any novels? ('Beckett is still alive'.)

Did Disraeli *write* any novels? ('Disraeli is now dead'.)

In all these examples, the period in question is assumed rather than named: it is the lifetime of the person or institution denoted by the subject of the sentence.

62 PRESENT RESULT. The resultative use of the Present Perfect (in BE) is shown in contrast to the Simple Past in:

Peter *has injured* his ankle ('His ankle is still bad').

Peter *injured* his ankle ('. . . but now it's better').

The second permits us (and in fact encourages us) to conclude that the result of the injury has disappeared.

a. On the other hand, the Simple Past is used for definite historical events, even when their results are still there: *This house was built by Inigo Jones*; *Tobacco was brought to England by Sir Walter Raleigh*.

b. In AE, for present result as for recent indefinite past, the Present Perfect can often be replaced by the Simple Past.

63 INDEFINITE TIME. Whereas the Present Perfect, in its indefinite past sense, does not name a specific point of time, a definite POINT OF ORIENTATION in the past ('then') is normally required (in BE) for the appropriate use of the Simple Past Tense. The point of orientation may be specified in one of three ways:

(a) by an adverbial expression of time-when:
I *saw* him *on Tuesday*.

(b) by a preceding use of a Past or Perfect Tense:
I *have seen* him already—he *came* to borrow a hammer.

(c) by implicit definition; i.e., by assumption of a particular time from the context:

Did you *put* the cat out? (said between husband and wife who have in mind a particular time when the cat is normally ejected).

DEFINITE AND INDEFINITE PAST MEANING

64 We need to elaborate a little more on the concept of definiteness.

The 'definite'/'indefinite' contrast between Simple Past and Present Perfect is exactly parallel to the contrast in meaning between the definite article *the* and the indefinite article *a* or *an*. We say *the cat* rather than *a cat* whenever a particular animal has already been mentioned, or else whenever, even though no cat has been mentioned, we know simply from shared familiarity with the context, what particular animal is under discussion. When husband says to wife *Did you put the cat out*?, it is clear to them both, without discussion, which cat is meant.

The two conditions of previous mention and uniqueness within the context correspond to conditions (b) and (c) in § 63 above.

A further resemblance is this. It is natural to start a conversation *indefinitely*, then to progress to *definite* reference (Past Tense, definite article, personal pronouns) once a frame of reference has been established:

> *A man* and *a woman* happened to be passing; *the man* suddenly turned round and threatened me; *he* said I had no right . . .

Similarly, Past follows Perfect:

> Joan *has received* a proposal of marriage; it *took* us completely by surprise.

> There *have been* times when I *wished* you were here.

> *A*: I*'ve* only *been* to Switzerland once. *B*: How *did* you like it? *A*: It *was* glorious—we *had* beautiful weather all the time.

After the definite time has been established, the Past Tense may of course be repeatedly used to denote events happening simultaneously or in succession, just as one may continue to refer to a person as *the man* or *he*.

a. Implicit definition can often be clarified by taking the corresponding indefinite statement as given by context, and by mentally reading in a *when* clause. *Who gave you this tie*?, for instance, can be expanded into the following train of thought: 'This tie has been given you by someone—that much I know already; but *when it was given you*, who gave it you?' Other examples are: *Did you have a good journey*? ('. . . when you came here'); *Did you enjoy your meal*? ('. . . when you ate it'); *I went to school with Ted Heath* ('. . . when I was a schoolboy').

b. When the topic of a sentence is unique (e.g. often when its subject or object is a proper name) the definiteness extends to the verb form, so that Past Tense is selected: in *Philadelphia was founded by William Penn*, the Past Tense is only natural, since we know that Philadelphia is a definite place, and was founded at a definite point in history. In this connection, it is interesting to contrast (in BE) the indefinite *John has painted* A *picture* with the definite *John painted* THIS *picture*.

c. The Past Tense, indicating a definite point of orientation in the past, is to be expected in temporal clauses introduced by *when, while, since*, etc., because the time specified in such clauses is normally assumed to be already given: *You made a mistake when you bought that dog*; *She hasn't spoken to us since we quarrelled about the will*. (*When* followed by the Present Perfect is not frequent, and must be understood in a past-in-the-future or habit-up-to-the-present sense.) If the *when* clause contains a Past Tense verb, the main clause must also be in the Past Tense, the *when* clause being classed as an adverbial expression of time-when equivalent to *last week*, *three years ago*, etc. (see § 69).

d. There is an idiomatic exception to the rule that the Simple Past Tense indicates definite meaning: this is the construction with *always* illustrated by *I always said he would end up in jail*; *Timothy always was a man of peace*. It is simply a colloquial variant of the Present Perfect with 'state verbs', and can always be replaced by the equivalent Present Perfect form. There are equivalent question and negative forms with *ever* and *never*: *Did you ever see such a mess*? *I never met such an important person before*.

e. The Present Perfect appears to be used less widely in AE than in BE, and in particular, it is quite common to hear in North America the Simple Past where in Great Britain the Present Perfect in its recent-indefinite-past sense would be standard: *Did you sell your tape-recorder yet*?

f. The Simple Past is sometimes used in comparative sentences where *used to*+Infinitive would be more generally appropriate (see § 84): *I'm not so young as I* WAS=*I'm not so young as I* USED TO BE.

MISCELLANEOUS POINTS

65   Although the meanings of the Simple Past and Present Perfect are different in the ways stated, it is worth bearing in mind that they are sometimes interchangeable. For example, a person who has mislaid his spectacles might exclaim either *Now where did I put my glasses*? or *Now where have I put my glasses*? The difference between these two is merely a slight difference of viewpoint: in the first sentence, the speaker's attention is fixed on the moment when he lost his glasses, in an effort to remember what he did at that time; in the second, he turns his attention to the present result of this action, and the question uppermost in his thoughts is 'Where are they now?'

66   Like the ordinary Present Tense, the Present Perfect can be used with reference to an imaginary 'present moment' (see § 25*b*):

John and Joy Jennings, who *have been fighting* a gang led by Red Reagan, *have followed* the sinister goatherd Khari to a mountain hide-out, where they *stumble* upon a coded message from Red's lieutenant, Hercule Judd . . .

In this way a writer of a children's serial story might give a retro-spective account of previous episodes, using the Present Perfect for events which are 'in the past' from the point of view of the stage of the story now reached.

67   The non-finite verb is strictly outside the subject-matter of this book, but one important point must be made about it. As the Past Tense belongs to finite verb constructions only, the Perfect form does duty, in non-finite constructions, for both Past Tense and Perfect Aspect. Thus it can have both definite and indefinite reference: *Having seen a doctor yesterday* shows the Perfect form of the present participle co-occurring with *yesterday* – something not allowable with a finite verb. Similarly with a *to*+Infinitive construction: *He is believed to* HAVE LEFT *last Monday* means practically the same as *It is believed that he* LEFT *last Monday*. The same point can be made, more relevantly, about the Infinitive in finite verb constructions with modal auxiliary verbs (see § 138): *He may* HAVE LEFT *last Monday* is equivalent to *It is possible that he* LEFT *last Monday*.

ADVERBIALS IN RELATION TO PERFECT AND PAST

68   All tenses of the English verb map time by means of points of orientation (or 'points of reference') which roughly indicate the relation of one time to another.

The primary point of orientation is either the present moment – the moment 'now' when the speaker is actually speaking, or (sometimes) the moment at which he imagines himself to be speaking. But with the Past Tense, there is a secondary point of orientation as well: as we have seen, it is an important difference between the Simple Past and Present Perfect that the Past indicates a past point of orientation 'then', whereas the Present Perfect relates past time more directly to the present point of orientation 'now'.

It is a consequence of this difference that the range of time adverb-ials (i.e., adverbs, adverbial phrases, and adverbial clauses) combining with the Past Tense is by no means the same as the list of time adverb-ials combining with the Present Perfect. We have already observed some of the differences; nevertheless, it will be useful at this point to summarise usage with regard to adverbials. A rough general rule is that with the Present Perfect as with Present Tenses in general,

D

adverbials must have reference, in one way or another, to the present point of orientation 'now', while with the Past Tenses they must refer to some point or period of time in the past.

69   Adverbials associated with the Past Tenses include *a week ago, earlier this year, last Monday, the other day, yesterday evening* (BE), and similar phrases. These, like the single adverb *yesterday*, refer to a specific time in the past, and so cannot occur with the Present Perfect.

At four o'clock, in the morning, on Tuesday, then, soon, next, after breakfast, etc. Members of this group, although they do not refer explicitly to the past, are most likely to be found with the Past Tense. With the Present Perfect, they can have only an indefinite or iterative sense, as in *He has always smoked in bed in the morning* (or . . . *in the mornings*).

70   In contrast, the following are adverbials associated with the Present Perfect rather than the Past:

So far, up to now, hitherto, since Thursday, since I met you, etc. Such phrases normally refer to a time period stretching up to 'now', and so have to go with the Present Perfect in its state, indefinite past, or habitual senses.

Lately and *latterly* (BE) normally go with the recent indefinite past interpretation of the Present Perfect.

For the present, for now, for the time being, etc. indicating present duration may accompany the Present Perfect, but not the Past.

a. Present time-when adverbials such as *nowadays* and *these days* cannot accompany either the Perfect Present or the Past; they require the Simple Present or Present Progressive.

71   The next group is comprised of adverbials combining with either the Present Perfect or the Past.

To-day, this month, this year, this century, etc. refer to a period including the present moment: with them, the Present Perfect and Past Tense are virtually interchangeable. If there is a difference of meaning between *I went to the dentist today* and *I have been to the dentist today*, it is that the second underscores the result aspect of the verb.

This morning, to-night, this March, this Christmas, etc. refer to a period which is part of a larger period including the present moment (as 'this morning', for instance, is part of 'today'). With *this morning/afternoon/evening*, it is sometimes said that the Present Perfect indicates

THE EXPRESSION OF PAST TIME   41

that the period referred to is not yet over—that, e.g., it is possible to say *I have been to the dentist this morning* at 11 a.m., but not at 3 p.m. This distinction, if made, accords with the principle that the Present Perfect has to involve a period extending up to the present. But other speakers of English claim it is possible to say *I've been to the dentist this morning* in the afternoon or evening: for them, it seems, we may interpret *this morning* as 'today in the morning'.

Phrases of calendar time such as *this March* conform to the general rule that a period that is gone requires the Past Tense: the most natural inference from *I saw him this March* is that March is over, while *I have seen him this March* suggests that March is still with us.

Recently and *just*, as adverbs of the near past, can take either the Present Perfect or the Past: *I've just seen your boy-friend* or *I just saw your boy-friend*. Other adverbials with 'recent' meaning are somewhat wayward in their behaviour: *lately* and *latterly* (as we saw in § 70 above) normally collocate with the Present Perfect; *just now*, on the other hand, is like *a moment/second/minute ago* in requiring the Past Tense.

With *always*, *ever*, and *never*, Past and Present Perfect are largely interchangeable when describing a period up to the present (see § 64*d*).

72 Finally, we turn to adverbials combining with either Perfect or Past but with a clear difference of meaning.

Now, as we would expect, is principally associated with the Present Tenses: *Now my ambition is/has been fulfilled*. With Past Tense, it is a narrative substitute for *then* (= 'at this point in the story'): *Now my ambition was fulfilled*.

Once with the meaning 'on a certain occasion, at one time', accompanies the Past Tense, despite its indefinite meaning: *I was once an honest man*. With the Present Perfect, it is a numerical adverb contrasting with *twice*, *three times*, etc.: *I have visited the Highlands only once*.

Already, *still*, *yet*, and *before* occur with the Present Perfect in the sense 'as early as now', 'as late as now', etc.: *I've seen him already*; *I still haven't seen him*. With the Past, they must have a meaning involving a past point of orientation: *I was already* (= 'as early as then') *very hungry*.

PAST PERFECT

73   The Past Perfect Tense (*I had written*, etc.) has the meaning of
past-in-the-past, or more accurately, 'a time further in the past, seen
from the viewpoint of a definite point of time already in the past'.
That is, like the Simple Past Tense, the Past Perfect demands an already
established past point of reference. This is why it is difficult to begin
a conversation with the Past Perfect Tense.

It would be unnecessary to give a separate account of the Past
Perfect if it were merely a question of adding the Perfect Aspect meaning to Past Tense meaning. But in fact the Past Perfect covers an area
of meaning (further in the past) equivalent to both the Past and Perfect.
It is like the Perfect Aspect of non-finite verbs (see § 67) in being capable of referring to both indefinite and definite time: contrast *The
parcel had already arrived* (indefinite) with *The parcel had arrived on
April 15th* (definite).

In discussing the Past Perfect, it is useful to distinguish between the
ordinary past point of orientation 'then' (T) and the previous point of
time 'before then' (B):

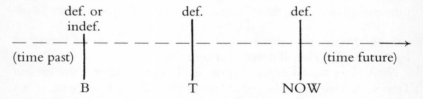

Whereas T (by its very nature as a point of orientation) is definite, B
is either definite or indefinite. The following examples show the Past
Perfect paralleling the functions of the Present Perfect as discussed in
§§ 55–59:

The house had been empty for ages (state-up-to-then, cf. § 55).

Had they been to America before? (indefinite past-in-past, cf. § 56).

Mr. Phipps had preached in that church for fifty years (habit-up-
to-then, cf. § 58).

The goalkeeper had injured his leg, and couldn't play (resultative
past-in-past, cf. § 59).

For *The parcel had arrived on April 15th*, however, there is no corresponding Present Perfect sentence, because a definite time B ('before
then') is mentioned.

It is worth noting that an adverbial of time-when with the Past Perfect can designate either T ('then') or B ('before then'):

When the police arrived, the thieves *had run away*.
The thieves *had run away* when the police arrived.

In the first of these sentences, the *when* clause identifies T, whereas in the second sentence it probably identifies B.

74   Similarly, it is worth noting that in some contexts, particularly following the conjunction *after*, the Simple Past and Past Perfect are interchangeable. These two sentences could well be describing the same sequence of events:

(1) I ate my lunch after my wife *had come* back from her shopping.

(2) I ate my lunch after my wife *came* back from her shopping.

After itself places the wife's arrival before the eating, so the Past Perfect is, in a way, redundant. What difference there is between these two statements can be represented as follows:

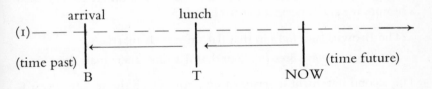

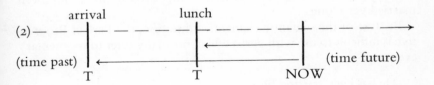

Statement (1) measures the 'beforeness' of the arrival from the event of eating lunch; statement (2) measures it directly from the present moment, treating it as another 'then', not as a 'before then'. (1) is the more usual choice.

From this illustration, we see that the fact that one happening is further in the past than another event already mentioned makes the use of the Past Perfect likely, but not necessary.

PERFECT PROGRESSIVE

75   Like the Past Perfect, the Perfect Progressive (*I have been working*, etc.) has a range of meaning that is not entirely predictable from the meanings of its components. Nevertheless, all feature of meaning associated with the Perfect Aspect and the Progressive Aspect considered separately come into play in one way or another.

76   The features associated with the Progressive in §§ 28–31 were DURATION, LIMITATION OF DURATION, and POSSIBLE INCOMPLETENESS. The first two of these give the Perfect Progressive its meaning of 'temporariness', seen in these examples:

I'*ve been writing* a letter to my nephew. | How *have* you *been getting* on? | It'*s been snowing* again.

The verbs here are 'activity verbs' which typically go with the Progressive Aspect. The meaning of the verbal form is roughly that of a TEMPORARY SITUATION LEADING UP TO THE PRESENT MOMENT, and is comparable to the state-up-to-the-present meaning of the non-progressive Present Perfect. There is, however, a difference between a temporary and a permanent time-scale:

The Browns *have lived* in that flat since their marriage.

The Browns *have been living* in that flat since their marriage.

The second statement describes a situation which the speaker regards as temporary; it therefore hints that the Browns have not been married very long.

Because of the semantic element of duration, the Perfect Progressive is difficult to use with verbs which normally refer to momentary events:

He has been starting his car.

*He has been starting his book.

The first of these makes sense, even though it reflects upon the reliability of the car. The second sentence, on the other hand, is non-sensical because it assigns duration to something which cannot have duration: the only way to make sense of it is to construe it as an ironical remark with the interpretation 'He has been meaning/trying/pretending to start his book'.

77   Two further differences between the Present Perfect Progressive and the ordinary Present Perfect with 'state verbs' are:

(A)   As examples above show, the Progressive need not be accompanied by an adverbial of duration. The sentence *It has snowed* without any adverbial qualification sounds very odd, while *It has been snowing* is quite permissible.

(B)   The Progressive may be used with many verbs which cannot be used with the non-progressive Present Perfect in this sense, because they cannot act as 'state verbs': *You've been reading that book for ages* is allowable, but not *You've read that book for ages*.

Once again, however, there is virtually a free choice between the two forms in many contexts: *Jack has been looking after the business for several years* and *Jack has looked after the business for several years* are equally correct.

a. There seems to be a tendency, particularly in colloquial English, to avoid the ordinary Present Perfect with verbs such as *sit, lie, wait*, and *stay*, which generally refer to temporary states. Thus *I've been sitting here all afternoon* is more idiomatic than *I've sat here all afternoon*. The same preference is exercised even with very long periods of time: *The inscription has been lying here for thousands of years* is more likely to be heard than *The inscription has lain here for thousands of years*.

b. The Perfect Progressive, however, is almost never found with the Passive Voice: *Volunteers have been running the organisation* could scarcely be turned into the Passive form of *The organisation has been being run by volunteers*. (One or two examples of such a construction, nevertheless, have been attested: perhaps this will be a future development of the English language.)

c. Naturally enough the non-progressive verb classes listed in § 37 do not normally appear with the Perfect Progressive: *I have been knowing Dr. Mason for some time* is unacceptable (see § 55a).

d. Although as a general rule a *since* clause requires the Present Perfect instead of the Simple Present (see § 7a), one may occasionally find a combination of *since* with the non-perfect Present Progressive in sentences such as *I am walking to work since my car broke down*. The normal construction is, however, the Present Perfect Progressive: *I have been walking to work since my car broke down*.

78   The element of POTENTIAL INCOMPLETENESS in the meaning of the Perfect Progressive comes to the attention when one thinks about the possibility of adding a statement predicting the continuation of the activity into the future:

He has been losing money for years ('. . . and will probably continue to lose money').

With verbs ('event verbs' and some 'activity' or 'process verbs') whose meaning entails eventual fulfilment or completion, the 'incompleteness' option in the Present Perfect Progressive contrasts crucially with the ordinary Present Perfect, which specifies that the conclusion has already been reached:

Who*'s been eating* my dinner? (? 'Some of it is left').
Who*'s eaten* my dinner? ('It's all gone').

They*'ve been widening* the road (? 'They're still at it').
They*'ve widened* the road ('The job's finished').

Where finality is not likely to be an issue, the two can be equally acceptable in the same situation. There is little to choose between *I've fed the chickens* and *I've been feeding the chickens*, except that the former places emphasis on the present accomplishment, the latter on the past activity.

79   Although 'present result' is not a part of the meaning of the Perfect Progressive in the examples above, in other circumstances there is a trace of it in the implication that THE EFFECTS OF THE ACTIVITY ARE STILL APPARENT:

You've been fighting again ('I can tell that from your black eye').

It's been snowing ('Look, the ground is white').

She's been crying again ('Look, her eyes are red').

In these cases, as in general with the Perfect Progressive, it is not necessary for the activity to continue right up to the present moment. Indeed, we frequently understand that THE ACTIVITY HAS RECENTLY STOPPED. The meaning-components 'effects still apparent' and 'recently finished' are closely connected, and it is very difficult to tell whether one of them is dependent on the other. Recentness is sometimes stressed by the adverb *just*: *I've just been listening to a programme on Vietnam.*

a. This element of meaning need not be in conflict with the element of 'non-completion'. *I've just been painting the house* implies 'I have recently stopped painting the house', but it may also mean that the job as a whole is incomplete and will be resumed later.

80   In summary, we may say that the main use of the Present Perfect Progressive combines elements 'continuation up to the present', 'recent indefinite past', and 'resultative past' found in the use of the non-progressive Present Perfect; and that in addition, it combines these with the concepts of temporariness and possible non-completion associated with the Progressive Aspect. Let us list these elements as follows:

The happening   (1) has duration
                (2) has limited duration
                (3) continues up to the present or recent past
                (4) need not be complete
                (5) may have effects which are still apparent.

81   Less commonly, the Present Perfect Progressive is also used in the iterative sense of TEMPORARY HABIT UP TO THE PRESENT: *He's been scoring plenty of goals this season.*

Examples can also be found of the second habitual meaning of the Progressive, that which involves stretching the time-span of each event rather than compressing the time-span of the habit as a whole (see § 50): *Whenever I have called, he has been mowing his lawn.*

PAST PERFECT PROGRESSIVE

82   The Past Perfect Progressive can be used in all the ways illustrated above with the Present Perfect Progressive, and what is more, may have the definite past-in-the-past meaning discussed in § 66; that is, it may be a shift further into the past of the meaning of the ordinary Past Progressive *was dancing* etc. Hence it is possible to join the Past Perfect Progressive, like the non-progressive Past Perfect, with an adverbial of time-when: *I had been speaking to him at 4 o'clock.* Hence, also, there is an ambiguity in the sentence *The inscription had been lying there for a thousand years:* this can mean (a) that the thousand years led up to 'then', the point of orientation (a use corresponding to the Present Perfect Progressive); or (b) that there was a gap between the thousand years and 'then' (a use corresponding to the ordinary Past Progressive).

FUTURE IN THE PAST

83   To balance the Past Perfect, one might expect the English language to possess a 'future in the past' tense for describing happenings which are in the future from some vantage point in the past. But there is no regular verbal construction with this meaning in everyday use.

Past Progressive forms or *was/were going to*+Infinitive with future reference are coloured by the notion of 'intention' (see § 92), and so do not guarantee that the event foreseen in the past actually did take place:

> The beauty contest *was taking place* on the next day.
> The beauty contest *was going to take place* on the next day.

To both of these one could add: 'This was the plan – but in fact it had to be cancelled because of bad weather'. These are therefore not true future-in-the-past tenses.

84   The language comes nearest to possessing a future-in-the-past tense in the constructions *would*+Infinitive and *was/were to*+Infinitive, when these are interpreted 'was/were destined to':

> Twenty years later, Dick Whittington *would be* the richest man in London.

> This strange, nervous individual *was* later *to be* defendant in one of the most notorious murder trials of all time.

Both these usages are uncommon, and are restricted to a literary style of historical writing or narrative. In neither case can the events fore-told be in the future from the *present* point of view of the narrator: they must take place between the 'then' of the narrative and the 'now' of the narration.

The use of these constructions in the sense 'was/were destined to' is so limited that in practice English speakers manage without a future-in-the-past construction, and use the ordinary Past Tense when they wish to anticipate some later event in past narrative: *Pitt, who later* BECAME *Britain's youngest Prime Minister, was at this time Chancellor of the Exchequer.*

a. Both *would*+Infinitive and *was/were to*+Infinitive are more commonly used in senses other than 'was destined to'. *Would*+Infinitive can be used as the equivalent of *will*+Infinitive in indirect speech, and indeed, the sentence about Dick Whittington above is ambiguous in that it is capable of construal not only in the 'was-destined-to' sense, but as free indirect speech, as if a parenthetic 'He said to himself' were added (see § 154). Likewise, *was to* may be the Past of *is to* in the sense of 'is due to', so that *Pitt was to be the next Prime Minister*, read in one way, is a prophecy, but read in another way, merely reports a plan which perhaps was never fulfilled (see § 144).

'USED TO'

85   Before we leave the subject of past time, there is the anomalous *used to* (pronounced /juːstu/or /juːstə/) + Infinitive construction to deal with. This construction indicates a past state (with 'state verbs'):

> Cigarettes *used to cost* two shillings a packet–now they cost three times as much. | That's the man who *used to be* organist of St. Paul's.

or else a past habit (with 'event verbs'):

> I *used to go* for a swim every day. | When I was young, my grand-father *used to tell* me stories of the Boer War.

Three points are to be noted about this construction.

(a)   *Used to* has no equivalent present construction *★uses to,* but because of its state or habit meaning, it typically points a contrast with a present state or habit, which can be expressed by a verb in the Simple Present: *I used to be rich* ('. . . but now I am poor').

(b)   *Used to* is not normally accompanied by an adverbial of time-when, but has its own 'built-in' adverbial *once* (='at one time'), in that the *used to* construction can be paraphrased by *once* with the Simple Past Tense:

> the man who *used to be* organist of St. Paul's=
> the man who *was once* organist of St. Paul's.

This clearly shows the element of 'indefinite past' normally present in the meaning of *used to*. Nevertheless, the combination of *used to* with an adverbial of time-when, if unusual, is not entirely unacceptable: *He used to live here in 1944.*

(c)   The 'indefinite past' meaning of *used to* forbids its combination with an adverbial naming the actual duration of the state or habit: *★He used to live here for twenty years.*

a. On the other hand, an adverbial of duration can be employed if it specifies the period of each event making up a habit: *He used to stay here for three days* is permissible, because *for three days* here refers to each of the series of occasions.

b. Used to never occurs with the Perfect Aspect: *★I used to have been working* *all afternoon*. With the Progressive Aspect, it is rare, but may be used in a habitual sense corresponding to that of § 50 'repetition of events of limited duration': *Often when I passed she used to be sitting there on the doorstep.*

Four

The Expression of Future Time

86 five ways of expressing future. 'WILL' AND 'SHALL': 87 prediction;
88 'll, will, and shall; 89 prophetic use; 90 past in future. 'BE GOING TO':
91 future fulfilment of the present; 92 future of present intention; 93 future
of present cause; 94 be going to inappropriate to most future conditional
sentences; 95 'imminence' not a necessary element of meaning; 96 does not
guarantee fulfilment of the event. PRESENT PROGRESSIVE WITH FUTURE
MEANING: 97–8 future of present plan, programme, or arrangement; 99
'imminence' frequently implied; 100 mainly restricted to 'doing' verbs.
SIMPLE PRESENT WITH FUTURE MEANING: 101 Simple Present with conditional
and temporal conjunctions; 102 future as 'fact'; 103 plan or arrangement
regarded as unalterable; 104 sequential use. 'WILL/SHALL'+PROGRESSIVE
INFINITIVE: 105 normal use; 106 'future as a matter of course'; 107 tactful
use; 108 interchangeability with will/shall+ Simple Infinitive. CONCLUDING
REMARKS: 109 list in order of importance; 110 list in order of certainty;
111 other methods of referring to the future; be about to.

86 There are a number of ways of expressing future time in English;
the most important of them are:

Will/shall+Infinitive: The parcel will arrive tomorrow.

Be going to+Infinitive: The parcel is going to arrive tomorrow.

Present Progressive: The parcel is arriving tomorrow.

Simple Present: The parcel arrives tomorrow.

Will/shall+Progressive Infinitive: The parcel will be arriving
tomorrow.

These verb forms all have their particular nuances of meaning, and
are far from being generally interchangeable. My task in this chapter
will be to explain the differences, beginning with the most common
construction, that of *will/shall* followed by the infinitive.

a *Shall* is little used as an alternative to *will* in AE.

'WILL' AND 'SHALL'

87 *Will* and *shall* have the double function of modal auxiliaries and auxiliaries of the future. The two functions are so closely intermingled that it is difficult to separate them. None the less, I shall try to deal with only the future function of the auxiliaries here, as far as possible leaving their volitional and other modal functions to the next chapter.

One reason for the confusion of future and modal uses of *will* and *shall* lies in the very nature of futurity. We cannot be as certain of future happenings as we are of events past and present, and for this reason, even the most confident prognostication must indicate something of the speaker's attitude and so be tinged with modality. *Will* and *shall* are no exception. The word which most usefully characterises the future meaning of *will* and *shall* is PREDICTION – something involving the speaker's judgement. Thus, although the *will/shall* construction provides English with its nearest approximation to a 'neutral' or 'colourless' future, one ought not to describe it as a 'future tense' on a par with the Past and Present Tenses.

88 The full auxiliary forms *will* and *shall* are frequently contracted in speech (especially after pronoun subjects) to the form written *'ll*, which may combine with subjects of all three persons to express future meaning:

> One day I'll die.
> One day you'll die.
> One day he'll die.

Shall, however, can express neutral predictive meaning only with a first-person pronoun as subject:

> One day I shall die. | One day we shall die.

With a second-person or third-person subject, *shall* has a modal meaning, which we discuss later (§§ 124–6); *you shall die* is a threat rather than a prediction in present-day English.

Will, like the contracted form *'ll*, is used with all three persons to express futurity:

> One day I will die.
> One day you will die.
> One day he will die.

With the first person pronouns, however, many English speakers feel that *shall* is the correct form, and so *I will* and *we will* are avoided in situations (such as in writing business letters) where people are on their best linguistic behaviour.

a. Shall is very occasionally found with second- and third-person subjects in an archaic, elevated style of prophetic utterance: *The earth shall be filled with God's glory*; *The time shall come when the poor and the oppressed shall rise against the oppressor.*

b. In AE, *I shall* and *we shall* are restricted to formal situations, as in the orator's *We shall never surrender.*

89   The *will/shall* future is used in a wide range of contexts in which it is appropriate to make predictions:

Tomorrow's weather *will be* cold and cloudy. | You *will feel* better after this medicine. | The next budget *will have to be* a severe one. | Perhaps I*'ll change* my mind after I've spoken to my wife.

Will/shall is particularly common in the main clause of conditional sentences:

If you pull this lever, the roof *will slide* back.

(In the *if* clause, however, the future condition is expressed by the ordinary Present Tense—see § 101).

As one might expect, the *will/shall* future is suitable for prophetic statements: *In twenty years' time, the average employee will work a twenty-five hour week.*

a. Will/shall can refer to either an indefinite or a definite time in the future: in *I shall keep my word, shall keep* is the future counterpart of the Present Perfect Tense (*I have kept my word*); in *Next year we shall have a good harvest, shall have* is the counterpart of the Simple Past. Frequently a sentence with *will/shall* is incomplete without an adverbial of definite time: *★It will rain*; *★The room will be cleaned.* These sentences are relatively unacceptable on their own, presumably because of their factual emptiness: we all feel certain that 'it will rain' at some time in the future, so there is no point in saying *★It will rain* unless an actual time can be forecast. *★It has rained* is odd for the same reason.

b. It will be taken for granted in the rest of this chapter that *will/shall*, and other methods of referring to future time, can be employed in reference to an imaginary narrative future: *Will John Jennings escape from the clutches of Red Reagan's gang? Find out in next week's* Conquest. (Cf. similar uses of Present and Present Perfect Tenses, §§ 25*b* and 66.) *Will/shall* is also often used on an imaginary time-scale in referring to a later part of a book or article: *We shall examine the sensory apparatus of bats and other nocturnal mammals in Chapter 25.*

90   *Will/shall* followed by the Perfect Infinitive is the usual means of expressing PAST IN FUTURE in English; i.e., of referring to a state or event seen in the past from a point of orientation in the future: *By next Wednesday, I'll have moved into the new house.* The time looked at retrospectively can either precede or follow the present moment, as is shown by the adverbials in this imaginary speech of a disgruntled student:

> By next week-end I'll be sick of exams; I'*ll have had* four exams *last week* and another four *in the coming week.*

There is a similar construction with the Perfect Progressive Infinitive:

> To-night the competitors *will have been driving* their cars continuously for twenty-four hours.

The 'future progressive' form *will be driving* etc., is discussed in §§ 105–8 below.

'BE GOING TO'

91   After *will/shall*, the next most important way of expressing future time is the construction *be going to* + Infinitive. If there is one general meaning that can be attached to this construction, it is FUTURE FULFILMENT OF THE PRESENT. In fact, however, it is useful to discriminate between two meanings, the FUTURE CULMINATION OF PRESENT INTENTION and the FUTURE CULMINATION OF PRESENT CAUSE.

a. Be going to + Infinitive here is an indivisible construction, not to be confused with a combination of the verb *go* with the infinitive of purpose. *I am going to see my grandmother on Saturday* can mean either 'I intend to see...' or 'I am going in order to see...'; the first alternative alone is our present concern.

92   The FUTURE OF PRESENT INTENTION is illustrated in these sentences:

> What *are* you *going to do* today? I'*m going to stay* at home and write letters. | Next year we'*re going to have* a holiday (AE *take* a vacation) abroad. | They'*re going to get* married in a registry office.

It is found chiefly with human subjects, and with 'doing' or 'agentive' verbs which imply conscious exercise of the will. Thus *I wonder if she's going to know you* strikes one as odd because one cannot will oneself into knowing somebody.

a. There is a slight difference of meaning, however, between *I am going to leave tomorrow* and *I intend to leave tomorrow*: the latter does not tell us whether the departure will take place or not; but *be going to* brings with it a strong expectation (if not quite a prediction) that the intention will be carried out. *I'm going to punish them* is stronger than *I intend to punish them* – it implies the speaker's confidence in his power to put the threat into effect.

b. The intention communicated by *be going to* is usually ascribable to the subject of the sentence – but not invariably. In passive sentences, it is often the intention of the implied agent that is in question: *This wall is going to be painted green* (= 'We or somebody else intend to paint this wall green').

93   The FUTURE OF PRESENT CAUSE is found with animal and inanimate subjects, as well as with human subjects; it is also common to both 'agentive' and 'non-agentive' verbs. It thus covers a wider range of contexts than the intentional meaning of *be going to*:

She's going to have another baby.
  (i.e. 'She's already pregnant')

I think I'm going to faint.
  ('I already feel ill')

There's going to be a storm in a minute.
  ('I can see the black clouds gathering')

In each of these there is the feeling that factors giving rise to the future happening are already present; or (to be meticulous) it is as if THE TRAIN OF EVENTS LEADING TO THE FUTURE HAPPENING IS ALREADY UNDER WAY. The first sentence may be contrasted with *She will have another baby*, which is the pronouncement of a soothsayer, rather than a piece of news.

From this, it is easy to see why *be going to* is often used in reference to the immediate future:

Watch it! That pile of boxes is going to fall!
  ('I can see it already tottering')

Look! He's going to score a goal!
  ('I can see him moving up to the goal-mouth')

Is going to score here is almost equivalent to *is about to score* or *is on the point of scoring*.

E

a. When the clause with *be going to* contains no time adverbial, immediate future is almost certainly indicated. *We're going to live in the country* implies, 'soon' unless some adverbial indicating otherwise, like *when we retire*, is added.

b. It is generally clear which of the two meanings of *be going to* applies to a given context, but ambiguities can arise: *He's going to arrive late at the concert* can mean either 'That is his intention' or 'That is what will happen, if he goes on like this'.

94   *Be going to* is inappropriate in most future conditional sentences:

If you accept that job, you*'ll* never *regret* it.
★If you accept that job, you*'re* never *going to regret it*.

The second of these sentences is unlikely because the eventuality described in the main clause in such sentences depends on future rather than present contingencies. *Be going to* is suitable, however, if present circumstances are mentioned in the *if* clause; i.e., if the condition is a present one rather than a future one: *We're going to find ourselves in difficulty if we carry on like this*.

95   In neither case is imminence a NECESSARY semantic accompaniment of *be going to*, as we see from the remote periods mentioned in in these statements:

Present intention: I*'m going to be* a policeman when I grow up.

Present cause or train of events: If Winterbottom's calculations are correct, this planet *is going to burn itself out* 200,000,000 years from now.

If one takes a fatalistic view of the future, of course, any coming event, however remote, may be thought to have its seeds in the present; and in any case, there is often in people's speech a sense of destiny vague enough to bring *be going to* almost as close to a neutral 'future tense' as *will/shall*. The two constructions can often be substituted for one another with little change of effect:

The whole idea of the digital computer *will be* obsolete in fifty years.
The whole idea of the digital computer *is going to be* obsolete in fifty years.

Will/shall can be replaced by *be going to* even more generally if the nearness of the event is signalled by an adverb, or is made clear by the situation:

What *will happen* now?= What *is going to happen* now?
Will you *be gone* long?= Are you *going to be gone* long?

Be going to is probably the more common choice when the event is in the near future.

96 *Be going to* does not guarantee that the anticipated happening will actually come to pass. This is illustrated most clearly with Past Tense examples:

He *was going to sue* me, but I persuaded him it was pointless. | The car *was going to crash*, but with the last wrench of the wheel I brought it to safety.

With the Past Tense, indeed, the usual interpretation is that fulfilment did not take place. Non-fulfilment is also characteristic of the Present Perfect version: *He's been going to mend that window-catch for months* ('. . . but he hasn't got round to it').

a. Be going to has no non-progressive alternant *⋆go to*, but otherwise has the full range of grammatically permissible tenses and aspects. The Infinitive part of the construction also varies for aspect, so that in theory 'double' Perfect and Progressive forms are possible: *I've been going to have finished the job by the time they arrive*; *They're going to be watching football next Saturday afternoon*. With a preceding *will/shall*, *going to* can express 'future in the future': *Call on me at lunchtime on Monday–I'll be going to speak to the boss about it that afternoon*. These complex constructions are on the whole very rare.

PRESENT PROGRESSIVE WITH FUTURE MEANING

97 Like *be going to*+Infinitive, the Present Progressive refers to a future happening anticipated in the present. But there is a subtle difference: it is not a present intention or cause, but rather a PRESENT ARRANGEMENT that is signalled by the Progressive.

98 A reasonably precise definition of the Progressive in this sense is: FUTURE EVENT ANTICIPATED BY VIRTUE OF A PRESENT PLAN, PROGRAMME OR ARRANGEMENT. Here are examples:

She*'s getting married* this spring. | Next they*'re playing* the Schubert Octet. | We*'re having* fish for dinner. | I*'m inviting* several people to a party.

In each there is the implication of an arrangement already made: the marriage has been fixed, the programme of music has been drawn up, the menu has been chosen, the party has already been decided on.

The difference between 'arrangement' and 'intention' is a very slight one; so *be going to* + Infinitive could be substituted for the Present Progressive in all these examples. There is, however, a change of emphasis, which is illustrated in this pair of sentences:

> I'*m going to take Mary out* for dinner this evening.
> I'*m taking Mary out* for dinner this evening.

An intention is part of one's present state of mind, while an arrangement is something already predetermined in the past, regardless of how the speaker feels now. Hence the second sentence, but not the first, could conceivably be uttered with some reluctance by someone who now regrets the arrangement – and it could very readily be used as an excuse: *I'm sorry, I'd like to have a game of billiards with you, but I'm taking Mary out for dinner.*

99   It is understandable that the notion of 'fixed arrangement' comes to be associated with the near rather than distant future. The element of IMMINENCE often accompanying the future use of the Present Progressive is amply illustrated in the examples just given, but as with *be going to*, the possibility remains of referring to the more remote future if it is regarded as determined in advance: *When I grow up, I'm joining the police force.*

A further point of resemblance between the Present Progressive and the *be going to* future is optionality of time adverbials. The following sentences without adverbial modification are in fact ambiguous out of context, as they may be given either a present (limited duration) or future (imminent) interpretation:

> I'*m taking* Mary out for a meal. | We'*re starting* a bridge-club. | The Smiths *are leaving.* | My aunt'*s coming* to stay with us. | He'*s resigning* from his job.

Without an adverbial, a time in the near future rather than remoter future is generally intended: one could insert the adverb *just* in some of these sentences to make the imminence explicit.

The use of the Present Progressive in this way seems to be chiefly limited to verbs of motion and some other verbs signifying single events. It is difficult, for example, to see any ambiguity in *I'm attending evening classes in Spanish*; because of its habitual meaning, this sentence must almost certainly refer to the present rather than the future, unless we add a future adverbial such as *next year*.

a. 'Transitional event verbs' such as *arrive*, *die*, *land* and *stop* in any case have an anticipatory element in their meaning when used with the Progressive Aspect (see § 35). *The aeroplane is landing*, *My train is stopping*, etc. are probably best regarded as exemplifying the present rather than the future use of the Present Progressive.

100   The factor of 'plan' or 'arrangement' in the future meaning of the Present Progressive restricts its use in the main to 'doing' verbs involving conscious human agency:

John *is rising* at 5 o'clock tomorrow.
★The sun *is rising* at 5 o'clock tomorrow.

The latter sentence is absurd because it suggests that the rising of the sun could be deliberately planned, instead of being determined by natural law. In this respect, the *be going to* future has wider application than the Present Progressive future: we can say *It is going to rain tomorrow* (a forecast on the basis of present circumstances), but not ★*It is raining tomorrow*.

a. This does not mean, however, that the Present Progressive is entirely limited to 'doing verbs'. In *I'm getting a present tomorrow*, the verb *get* is ambiguous—it can have either the active, agentive meaning 'acquire', or the passive, inert meaning 'receive'. The passive meaning is possible because in this case the plan is understood to have been made and carried out by someone other than the subject of the sentence: the meaning is approximately 'Someone has arranged to give me a present tomorrow'.

b. A further, predictable restriction on the future use of the Present Progressive is that it does not occur with verbs (such as *to be*, see § 37G) that are normally incompatible with the Progressive Aspect: we could very well ask *Who is going to be captain of the team next Saturday?*, but not ★*Who is being captain of the team next Saturday?*

SIMPLE PRESENT WITH FUTURE MEANING

101   In dependent clauses introduced by conditional and temporal conjunctions *if*, *unless*, *when*, *as soon as*, *as*, etc., the future is denoted by the ordinary Present Tense instead of the construction with *will/shall*:

I'll tell you if it *hurts*. | When the spring *comes*, the swallows will return. | Jeeves will announce the guests as they *arrive*.

It can be argued that this is not just a requirement of the syntactic pattern, but has its basis in a contrast of meaning. In the dependent clauses mentioned, the happening referred to is not a prediction, but a fact that is taken as given. A conditional sentence, for instance, has the structure 'If X is a fact, then I predict Y'. Hence in the *if* clause it is appropriate to use the Present Tense, with its assumption of factual certainty, rather than the predictive auxiliary *will* or *shall*.

a. Notice the following ambiguity: in the sentence *If you love me, we shall be happy*, the *if* clause can mean either 'love me now' or 'love me in the future'.

b. When *will* appears in a dependent conditional or temporal clause, it requires a volitional interpretation, because (as we have just seen) the sense of 'prediction' is not available in that position: *If you will* (i.e. 'are willing to') *love me, we shall be happy*.

102   The key to the Simple Present as a 'future tense' is, then, that it represents FUTURE AS FACT; that is, it attributes to the future the same degree of certainty that we normally accord to present or past events. Outside adverbial clauses, statements about the calendar are the most straightforward illustrations:

Tomorrow *is* Saturday. | Next Christmas *falls* on a Thursday.

But any aspect of the future which is regarded as immutable may be similarly expressed:

The term *starts* on 23rd April. | Next year the United Nations *celebrates* the twenty-fifth anniversary of its Charter. | The train *leaves* at 7.30 this evening.

Since most future happenings are in principle subject to doubt, the Simple Present Tense, which describes a future event by a categorical statement of fact, is in general a special or 'marked' form of reference which overrides the normal feeling that the future is less certain than the present or past. A statement like *Next week John fails his exams* is unthinkable except as an ironical comment, suggesting that John's failure is as sure as the rising of the sun, or the fact that Wednesday will succeed Tuesday.

103   From this it is an easy step to the Simple Present signifying a PLAN OR ARRANGEMENT REGARDED AS UNALTERABLE:

We *start* for Istanbul to-night. | I *get* a lump sum when I retire at sixty-five. | Her case *comes* before the magistrate next week. | The Chancellor *makes* his budget speech tomorrow afternoon.

The Simple Present is a 'marked' future here also: it carries a special, rather dramatic overtone similar to that of the 'instantaneous present' (see § 10). It would weaken the force of the above sentences to substitute the Present Progressive: *We are starting for Istanbul to-night* announces a present plan which may, conceivably, be altered later; but in *We start for Istanbul to-night* changing the plan is out of the question.

A further difference between the two constructions is that the arrangement conveyed by the Present Progressive is generally (but not necessarily) assumed to have been made by the subject of the sentence. *I am starting to-night* almost always means '*I* have arranged to start to-night'. But with the Simple Present, the arrangement is often felt to be an impersonal or collective one—made, for example, by a committee, a court of law, or some un-named authority.

a. Not that this difference is always felt: *The match starts at two o'clock* and *The match is starting at two o'clock* are more or less equivalent statements, as in both one supposes that it is the organisers of the match that have made the arrangement.

104 In its future use, the Simple Present refers to a definite future occasion in the same way as the Simple Past Tense (see § 64) refers to a definite occasion in the past. This means it must be accompanied by an adverbial referring to future time, unless it occurs in a narrative sequence, or in a context where some definite point of time in the future is assumed. An example of such a narrative sequence is:

Right! We *meet* at Victoria at nine o'clock, *catch* the fast train to Dover, *have* lunch at the Castle Restaurant, then *walk* across the cliffs to Deal.

The tone of this statement, as well as suggesting an irrevocable decision to follow the stated programme, also has something in common with the 'dramatic present' of stage directions (see § 25*a*): it is as if the speaker enacts in advance the events as they will take place.

a. A related use of the Simple Present is the melodramatic expression of inexorable determination in *One more step, and I* SHOOT *you!*—a style of threat beloved of writers of popular crime and adventure stories. Compare also the imperative use of the Simple Present with the inversion of Verb and Adverbial Complement in *Into bed you go! Down you get!* Such commands have a rather condescending air, and are used mainly in addressing pets and young children.

b. Note the two meanings of *His train leaves at five o'clock*, which can indicate either future (=‘. . . at five o'clock to-day’) or habitual present (=‘at five o'clock every day’).

c. The Simple Present in reference to a predetermined plan normally demands a ‘doing verb’; the unacceptability of *You know the answer next month* springs from the status of *know* as a ‘verb of inert cognition’ (see § 37F).

‘WILL/SHALL’+PROGRESSIVE INFINITIVE

105   The construction *will/shall be working*, according to the general rules for the use of Progressive Aspect, can refer to temporary situations in the future (see §§ 28–31):

> This time next week I *shall be sailing* across the Atlantic. | Don't phone me at seven o'clock – I *shall be eating* my supper.

Moreover, as these examples show, the action is typically associated with a future point of time round which it forms a ‘temporal frame’ (see § 32). In this, the ‘future progressive’ with *will* is like the Past Progressive and habitual Present Progressive.

106   There is also, however, an independent use of *will/shall*+ Progressive: a use which applies to a single event viewed in its entirety (and therefore without the characteristic ‘framing effect’). This use requires separate notice, as it is not just a question of combining the predictive meaning of *will/shall* with the meaning of the Progressive Aspect. Examples are:

> The train *will be arriving* at eight o'clock. | I *shall be writing* to you soon. | When *will* you *be moving* to your new house?

The meaning of the verbal construction here is perhaps the most difficult of all future meanings to characterise. It can be roughly summed up in the phrase FUTURE-AS-A-MATTER-OF-COURSE, and indicates that a predicted event will happen independently of the will or intention of anyone concerned.

It is tempting to speculate that this usage has grown up through the need to have a way of referring to the future uncontaminated by factors of volition, plan, and intention which enter into the future meanings of *will/shall*+Infinitive, the Present Progressive, and *be going to*+Infinitive.

Although the volitional uses of *will/shall* have not so far been discussed (see § 123–4 below), it is important to notice here that with human subjects and 'agentive' or 'doing' verbs, *will/shall* frequently combines prediction with overtones of volition (see § 123C, 124C). Hence there is a clear distinction of meaning in these pairs:

{ (a) *I'll drive* into London next week (I've made up my mind').
{ (b) *I'll be driving* into London next week ('as a matter of course').

{ (c) *Will* you *put on* another play soon? ('Please!')
{ (d) *Will* you *be putting on* another play soon? ('Is this going to happen?')

In principle, it is possible to use (a) in the neutral predictive sense of *I shall die one day*; but in practice, it is difficult to avoid suggesting at the same time that one *wants and intends* to drive to London. The possibility of volitional colouring is avoided in sentence (b), which is understood simply as a statement that 'such-and-such is going to happen'. The same thing applies to the second pair. As a question, sentence (c) implicates the intentions of the listener, and therefore comes to sound almost like a cajoling imperative; but sentence (d) simply asks whether a further production will come to pass.

a. To illustrate the difference between the regular and special meanings to the *will/shall* + Progressive construction, notice that the following sentence may be interpreted either with or without the 'framing effect': *I shall be visiting my aunt at six o'clock.*

b. The 'matter-of-course' meaning does not seem to occur with 'state verbs', as is argued by the lack of ambiguity of a sentence like *We'll be living in London next year.*

107   One reason why the *will/shall* + Progressive usage has become quite common in everyday speech is that it is often a more polite and tactful alternative to the non-progressive form. Sentence (b) above could easily precede the offer *Can I give you a lift?*, for it would forestall any awkward feeling of indebtedness on the listener's part: 'I shall be making the journey anyway, so don't feel you would be causing me trouble'. Similarly, sentence (d) expresses polite interest in the future theatrical programme, while avoiding any suggestion of putting pressure on the person questioned.

108   The negative, disclaiming element in the *will/shall* + Progressive form does not, however, give an explanation of all cases of this usage.

It is possible to find sentences which differ little in meaning from their non-progressive counterparts:

The sun *will set* in a minute.
The sun *will be setting* in a minute.

In neither sentence is there any question of personal involvement, so the 'matter-of-courseness' which makes a significant contrast in the case of 'doing verbs' has little distinctive value.

a. The 'matter of course' connotation helps to account for a temporal restriction which commentators have noted in the *will/shall*+Progressive construction: viz., that it generally refers to the near, but not too immediate future. If we think of the underlying notion 'this will happen in the natural course of events', we shall not expect it to refer to events too far in the future nor to events too close at hand. This general rule has exceptions, however: one does come across sentences indicating the very imminent future, like *The train will be leaving in a second.*

b. A second restriction consists in the avoidance of this Progressive form in describing abnormal or sudden or violent events which could not be said to happen 'in the natural course of things'. Remarks like *Margot will be poisoning her husband when he gets home* or *We shall be blowing up the Houses of Parliament to-night* have a crazy, semi-comic air which arises from the incongruity of treating such outrages as 'matter of course'. On the other hand, it is intriguing to note that there is an idiomatic exploitation of such incongruities in colloquial English: *You'll be losing your head one of these days* (said to a very forgetful person) or *He'll be buying himself an island in the Bahamas next* (said to someone aspiring to a life of luxury). The message (with allowance for a certain amount of comic hyperbole) runs: 'This is what things will come to in the natural course of events if he carries on in this absurd way'. In the same spirit of comic exasperation is the commonly-heard question *Whatever will he be doing next?*

CONCLUDING REMARKS

109   I would place the five types of 'future tense' listed at the beginning of this chapter in the following order of importance:

(1)   *will/shall*+Infinitive

(2)   *be going to*+Infinitive

(3)   Present Progressive

(4)   *will/shall*+Progressive Infinitive

(5)   Simple Present.

Probably the most significant point to notice is the relative infrequency of the Simple Present Tense as an expression of future time, in comparison with the corresponding construction in other prominent European languages.

110   Another list, this time ordering according to the degree of certainty ascribed to the future happening, may also help to give guidance on the choice of 'future tense':

(1) Simple Present (most certain)

(2) $\begin{cases} will/shall + \text{Infinitive} \\ will/shall + \text{Progressive Infinitive} \end{cases}$

(3) $\begin{cases} be\ going\ to + \text{Infinitive} \\ \text{Present Progressive} \end{cases}$ (least certain)

Even those marked 'least certain', however, convey at the least a strong expectation of the future event.

111   There are further ways of expressing future time, such as *be about to* + Infinitive and *be destined to* + Infinitive, but of these only *be about to* is common enough to be worth comment. This construction refers to the immediate future, and is thus sometimes a near equivalent to *be going to* or the Present Progressive: *He was about to strike me* (= 'He was going to strike me'); *They are about to leave* (= 'They are leaving').

Five

The Modal Auxiliaries

112 Many pages, chapters, even books, have been written about the modal auxiliary verbs in English. What makes it so difficult to account for the use of these words (which may be called 'modal auxiliaries' or 'modals' for short) is that their meaning has both a logical and a practical (or pragmatic) element. We can talk about them in terms of such logical notions as 'permission' and 'necessity', but this done, we still have to consider ways in which these notions become remoulded by the psychological pressures which influence everyday communication between human beings: factors such as condescension, politeness, tact, and irony. Condescension, for example, intervenes to make the *may* of *You may go* (which in logical terms means no more than 'permission') into something approaching a command (see § 113A*b*).

These factors do not influence only the modals: one can compare the way in which *Would you mind . . .?* and *Would you like . . .?*, at face value questions about the listener's inclinations, are frequently used as polite commands.

This chapter will begin with a listing (as in a dictionary) of the meanings of the six verbs *may, can, must, have to, will,* and *shall,* together with an account of the contrasts and similarities between them. I shall try to show that the English language is far more consistent and 'rational' in its expression of modal meanings than has generally been supposed.

Later, attention will be turned to the relation between the Present Tense forms *may, can,* etc. and the Past Tense forms *might, could,* etc. It is as well to bear in mind, however, that 'present' and 'past' are misleading titles for these forms. The Present Tense auxiliaries might more properly be called 'non-past', as they refer to future as well as to present time (see § 135). The Past Tense auxiliaries, on the other hand, have various other functions, apart from that of indicating past time: some of these functions will be postponed until Chapter 7.

The meanings of the modals as stated below apply primarily to positive statements; negative and question forms on the whole have to be separately considered.

a. In grammatical terms, *have to* is not an auxiliary verb on the same footing as the others: it has, for example, an infinitive form, which means that it can combine with other modals (as in *We may have to go*) and can combine with *will/shall* to express future time: *We'll have to go*. Nevertheless, it cannot be semantically separated from *may, must,* and *can*.

'MAY'

113 The chief meanings of *may* are:

A. PERMISSION [GIVEN BY THE SPEAKER]

You may smoke in this room ('You are permitted [by me] to smoke in this room'). | Residents may use the car-park without a ticket.

In colloquial English, *may* characteristically signals permission given by the speaker. In more formal contexts, however, the meaning is not limited in this way, but is extended to GENERAL PERMISSION without respect to who does the permitting. In formal English, that is, *may* replaces *can* (§ 114B), which is often considered less polite and less 'correct' than *may*. A guide-book might say *Visitors may ascend the tower for sixpence*, preferring *may* to *can*, which would be more natural in conversation.

a. In questions and *if* clauses (see §§ 127, 127*b*) *may* typically indicates permission given not by the speaker, but by the person questioned. *May I smoke?* thus means 'Will *you* allow me to smoke?' rather than 'Will *I* permit myself to smoke?', clearly an odd question to ask. The shift from first-person to second-person as the source of authority is also found with *must* and *shall* (see §§ 115 A*a*, 127).

b. *You may go, Jones* (spoken, typically, by a schoolmaster in an old-fashioned schoolboy story) is an instance of the strengthened, almost imperative use of *may*. The suggestion is that so great is the speaker's authority that merely for him to grant permission for something is a guarantee of its instant execution. Perhaps it is because of its association with the authoritarianism of the Victorian schoolmaster that this use of *may* is now less used.

c. In colloquial AE, and to a lesser extent in colloquial BE, *may* (= 'permission') seems to be losing ground to the more popular form *can*.

B. POSSIBILITY

Careful, that gun may be loaded. ('It is possible that it is loaded'). | You may lose your way if you don't take a map. | I may have misunderstood you.

This use of *may* is common in statements; it does not occur, however, in questions.

May in the 'possibility' sense is stressed, whereas in the sense of 'permission' it is usually unstressed. Thus the ambiguity, on paper, of a sentence like *He may leave tomorrow* ('permission' or 'possibility'?) rarely arises in speech.

May in this, as in the previous sense, usually refers to a future event when combined with an 'event verb': *may go, may become, may lose*, etc. (see § 135).

a. The 'permission' and 'possibility' meanings are close enough to one another for the distinction to be blurred on occasions. It is particularly easy to confuse them in scientific and mathematical writing where the author is expounding an abstract system of thought. *May* in such circumstances could mean either 'This is what is permitted by the rules of the system' or

'This is what is possible within the system'. Statements about language often have this ambivalence, as well: *Transitive verbs may be active or passive.* Does this mean 'The rules of English permit transitive verbs . . .' or 'It is possible that transitive verbs . . .'? In practice, in such a context there is little difference.

b. We should not conclude from Note *a*, however, that the 'permission'/'possibility' distinction is unreal. There are important grammatical differences between the two senses of *may*. Only the 'permission' sense, for example, is found in questions; only the 'permission' sense allows (in BE not AE) the contraction *mayn't* (see §132*a*); and the negation of the 'permission' sense (='I do not permit you . . .') is different in kind from that of the 'possibility' sense (='It is possible that . . . not . . .') (see § 132).

c. Writers of academic literature are fond of impersonal phrases such as *It may be noted . . .* , *we may consider . . .* It is particularly difficult to say whether 'permission' or 'possibility' is intended here. These rather empty formulae are simply pointers for the reader's attention.

d. On the difference between *can* and *may* as means of expressing 'possibility', see § 121.

e. Note the colloquial concessive use of *may* (='possibility') in remarks like: *She may not be pretty, but at least she knows her job* (='Whatever one thinks of her looks, she knows her job').

f. In AE, there is an apparent tendency to prefer *might* (see § 175) to *may* in expressing present possibility.

C. BENEDICTION AND MALEDICTION

May his evil designs perish! | May God grant you happiness!

This third exclamatory use of *may* is very formal, and is rarely found in modern English. It is marked by inversion of the subject and auxiliary verb. There are no interrogative, negative, or Past Tense forms.

'CAN'

114   The meanings of *can* are:

A. ABILITY

Our team can easily beat your team (='. . . is capable of . . ., . . . is able to . . .'). | I can resist everything except temptation. | Can you ride a horse?

Can in this sense is very common indeed, and is more or less synonymous with *is able to* or *is capable of*. When it refers to a permanent accomplishment (as in *Can you speak English?*), *can* is also more or less equivalent to *know how to.*

a. With verbs of 'inert perception' and 'inert cognition' (§§ 37E, 37F) there is really no difference between ability and accomplishment, so *can* tends to lose its distinctive modal meaning. *I can remember* scarcely differs from *I remember* as a means of indicating a state of recall. Similarly, there is little difference between *I can't understand* and *I don't understand*. With 'verbs of inert perception', on the other hand, *can* not only loses its modal value, but has the additional special function of denoting a state rather than an event. As the Simple Present with these verbs has only an 'instantaneous' meaning (see § 37Ea), the main difference between *I can hear* and *I hear, I can see* and *I see,* etc. is one of 'state of perception' versus 'momentary perception'.

B. PERMISSION

> You can smoke in this room. (='You are allowed to . . .'). | Residents can use the car-park without a ticket. | Can I borrow your pen?

Linguistic law-makers of the past have considered *may* to be the 'correct' auxiliary of permission, and have condemned the use of *can* for that purpose. Many an English schoolchild has been rebuked for saying *Can I . . .?* instead of *May I . . .?* Yet in fact, *can* is more widely used than *may* as an auxiliary of permission in colloquial English, having the less specific meaning 'you have permission' rather than '*I* give you permission'. *You can smoke in this room* means simply 'The rules allow it'. One can easily imagine the following conversational exchange with *can*, but not with *may*:

> MR. X: Can I smoke in here?
> MR. Y: So far as I know you can—there's no notice to the contrary.

On the other hand, *can* tends to be avoided in formal and polite usage (in both written and spoken English), because *may* is felt to be the more respectable form.

In colloquial speech, the difference between *can* and *may* is unimportant enough to be ignored in most cases.

a. The meaning of 'permission' is strengthened to something like 'strong recommendation' in *You can forget about your holiday*; *If he doesn't like it, he can lump it; You can jump in the lake,* and other more or less offensive remarks of the same kind. A possible explanation of the impolite tone of *can* here is that it brings with it a touch of irony: the speaker sarcastically offers someone the choice of doing something that cannot be avoided, or something no one would choose to do anyway.

C. POSSIBILITY

> Even expert drivers can make mistakes ('It is possible for even . . .'). |
> He can't be working at this hour! ('It is impossible . . .!') | Lightning
> can be dangerous.

This use of *can* is not particularly frequent in positive statements,
where it is in competition with *may* (§ 113B); but it is common in
negative and interrogative clauses. Often *can* (= 'possibility') can be
roughly paraphrased by the use of the adverb *sometimes*:

> Even expert drivers can make mistakes = Even expert drivers
> sometimes make mistakes.

a. It is not always easy to distinguish *can* (= 'possibility') from *can* (= 'ability')
as discussed in A. above. The two meanings are especially close, because
'ability' implies 'possibility' – that is, if someone 'is able to' do X, then X in
a sense is 'possible'. However, as *can* (= 'ability') and *can* (= 'permission')
require a human or at least animate subject, the 'possibility' sense is the only
one available when the subject is inanimate, as in *Lightning can be dangerous*.
Another distinguishing mark of the 'possibility' meaning is its occurrence
in passive clauses: *This game can be played by young children* means 'It is
possible for this game . . .'; but the corresponding active sentence *Young
children can play this game* could be interpreted in the 'ability' sense.

b. Colloquially, *can* (= 'possibility') is very often used to express a suggestion for future action: *We can see about that tomorrow*. In fact with second-
and third-person subjects, it has come to be a familiar though tactful
imperative – the type of imperative that might be used by the captain of a
team to his team-mates, or by a theatrical producer to his cast: *Mike and
Willy, you can be standing over there; and Janet can enter from behind that curtain*.
It is as though the speaker does not like to exert his authority openly by
using a direct imperative; so, counting on the co-operation of his hearers,
he merely suggests that a certain plan of action is POSSIBLE. This is a democratic imperative, to be used in addressing a person regarded as one's equal;
as such, it may be contrasted with the undemocratic coercive use of *shall*
(see § 124B). This *can* occurs with the Progressive Aspect (*you can be
standing* . . .), which is a sign that it belongs to the 'possibility' rather than
to the 'permission' sense (see § 139).

'MUST'

115 The meanings of *must* are:

A. OBLIGATION OR COMPULSION [IMPOSED BY SPEAKER]

> You must be back by ten o'clock ('You are obliged [by me] to . . .'). |
> Tell him he must stop this dishonest behaviour. | I must go now, or
> I'll be late.

F

A usual implication of *must*, as of *may* (='permission'), is that *the speaker is the person in authority*: he is the one who gives the orders. Consistent with this principle, *I must* and *we must* convey the idea of SELF-COMPULSION: the speaker exerts power over himself, perhaps through a sense of duty, through self-discipline, or merely through a sense of expediency.

a. Like *may* (§ 113A), *must* in questions and *if* clauses involves the hearer's authority instead of that of the speaker: *Must I answer all these letters myself?* means 'Are these your orders?'. In this connection, we may note a special sarcastic use of *must* with *you*: *'Must you make that dreadful noise?* ('For heaven's sake stop it!'); *If you 'must behave like a savage, at least make sure the neighbours aren't watching.* Remembering that *must* here indicates compulsion by the hearer (i.e. self-compulsion), we may see in this an element of petulant irony, as if the speaker pays lip-service to the idea that the hearer does what he does under internal compulsion rather than of his own free will. *If you 'must smoke, use an ash-tray* could be expanded 'If you are under compulsion to smoke (but of course you aren't—smoking is just a nasty habit you could break if you wanted to) . . .'. *Must* in such sentences could easily be replaced by *will* in the sense of 'insistence' (see § 123B), and like *will* in that sense, is invariably stressed.

B. LOGICAL NECESSITY

He must be working late at the office ('That is necessarily the case— no other explanation is possible'). | There must be some mistake. | You must have left your handbag in the theatre.

Must is used here of knowledge arrived at by inference or reasoning rather than by direct experience: for each example we could add the comment 'Given the evidence, there can be no other conclusion'. In each case, too, a chain of logical deduction can be postulated. For *I must be dreaming*, the stream of thought could run something like this: 'Here I am watching a fight between a lion and a unicorn; now, unicorns do not exist; therefore, the unicorn I see cannot be real; therefore, I cannot really be watching it; therefore I MUST be dreaming'.

This use of *must* normally has no negative or question form.

a. There is an understandable feeling that knowledge acquired indirectly, by inference, is less certain than knowledge acquired by direct experience. Hence 'logical necessity' can easily become weakened to 'logical assumption'. This weakening is evident in remarks like *You must be Mr. Jones* (i.e. 'I assume/I take it that you are Mr. Jones') or *You must be tired*. There is a more drastic weakening in estimating statements like *You must be a foot taller than I*; *He must be well over eighty*: these express little more than a guess.

'HAVE (GOT) TO'

116   The meanings of *have (got) to* correspond to those of *must*. The variant with *got* is generally substitutable for the one without *got* in colloquial BE, except that there are no non-finite forms ★*(to) have got to*, ★*having got to*. (*Have got to* is less used in the U.S.A.) Thus *got* cannot be inserted in the following: *We may have to leave early*; *I regret having to refuse your offer*.

A. OBLIGATION OR COMPULSION

You have to be back by ten o'clock ('You are obliged . . .'). | She'll have to sleep in the kitchen. | Pensioners have (got) to be careful with their money.

The meaning of *have (got) to* here differs from sense A of *must* in that the authority of the speaker is not involved: *have (got) to* conveys obligation generally, without specifying who does the compelling.

B. (LOGICAL) NECESSITY

There has to be some reason for his absurd behaviour ('That is necessarily the case – no other explanation is possible'). | Somebody had to lose the game (said in consolation to an unlucky card-player). | There has to be some mistake.

Have (got) to is less usual than *must* in the 'logical necessity' sense; the exact difference of meaning between them is explained in § 122.

a. *Have to* possesses question and negative forms both with and without the auxiliary *do*: *Do you have to go now? Have you to go now?* Up to recently, the first has been regarded as the usual American form, and the second as the usual British form. Now, however, the form with *do* is being increasingly used in the United Kingdom, and the second is becoming restricted to formal usage verging on the stilted. The forms *have . . . got to?* and *haven't got to* are common in colloquial British English.

b. The two different meanings of *have (got) to* are scarcely distinguishable in scientific and mathematical writing, for the same reason that applies to the different meanings of *may*, as explained in § 113Ba. To take a linguistic example: *Every clause has to contain a finite verb* could be interpreted either 'Every clause is obliged (by the rules of the language) to contain a verb', or 'It is necessary for every clause to have a verb'. In cases like this, the boundary between 'obligation' and 'necessity' is a fine one.

RELATIONS BETWEEN 'MAY', 'CAN', 'MUST', AND 'HAVE TO'

117 What must be clear by now is that there are close relations of meaning between the four verbs *may, can, must,* and *have to*. In fact, the relationships between all four can be precisely summarised in the diagram:

Permission/ Possibility	MAY	MUST	Obligation/ Necessity
	CAN	HAVE TO	

May and *can* share the same box because both express 'permission' and 'possibility'; *must* and *have* (*got*) *to* likewise both express 'obligation' and '(logical) necessity'. But in few cases are two verbs actually interchangeable: there is generally some slight difference of meaning. When we come to ask the question 'What are these slight differences?', it will be seen that *may* is in the same relation to *can* as *must* is to *have* (*got*) *to*.

118 First, however, there is another question to be answered: 'What of the horizontal relation of meaning between the left-hand box and the right-hand box?'. There is a special kind of meaning–contrast between 'permission' and 'obligation', and between 'possibility' and 'necessity': this 'oppositeness' we may call INVERSENESS (the two senses may be imagined as two sides of the same coin). So:

'permission' is the inverse of 'obligation'
'possibility' is the inverse of 'necessity'

What is meant by 'inverse' is made clearer by these equations:

(1) Some students *may stay out* after eleven o'clock=Not all students *have to be in* by eleven o'clock

(2) Someone *has to be telling lies*=Not everyone *can be telling the truth*

Pair (1) shows the connection between 'permission' and 'obligation'; pair (2) shows a similar connection between 'possibility' and '(logical) necessity'. Further, this interesting relationship of meaning is reversible: exchanging the positions of subject and predicate in pair (1), we arrive at another pair of sentences with the same logical meaning:

Some students have to be in by eleven o'clock = Not all students may stay out after eleven o'clock

A great deal more could be said about logical relations of this kind; but let us now return to the question of the slight differences of meaning between *may* and *can*, *must* and *have (got) to*.

119   Limiting attention now to 'PERMISSION' and 'OBLIGATION', we may recall that in the separate treatments of *may* and *must* (§§ 113A, 115A), both typically implicated the speaker as the person in authority. These observations may now be brought together and shown to fit into a regular pattern:

	The speaker has authority	
Permission	MAY	MUST	Obligation
	CAN	HAVE TO
	The authority comes from no particular source	

120   There is a similar pattern of likeness and contrast with the same auxiliaries in the senses of 'POSSIBILITY' and 'NECESSITY'. This time, however, the difference of meaning represented by the vertical dimension is that of FACTUAL versus THEORETICAL meaning:

	factual	
Possibility	MAY	MUST	(Logical) necessity
	CAN	HAVE TO
	theoretical	

The factual/theoretical contrast will be dealt with at greater length in Chapter 7 (§§ 157-8). At this point, it may be helpful to think of *may* and *must* as expressing the possibility or necessity of a FACT while *can* and *have (got) to* express the possibility or necessity of an IDEA.

121 The opposition of FACTUAL POSSIBILITY and THEORETICAL POSSIBILITY can be clarified by the following sets of equivalent statements:

FACTUAL: The road may be blocked=
                It is possible that the road is blocked=
                Perhaps the road is blocked

THEORETICAL: The road can be blocked=
                It is possible for the road to be blocked=
                It is possible to block the road

As we see, *may* is paraphrased by *It is possible* followed by a *that*-clause, but *can* is paraphrased by *It is possible* followed by a *for*+Noun Phrase +*to*+Infinitive construction.

The second sentence describes a theoretical conceivable happening, whereas the first feels more immediate, because the actual likelihood of an event is being considered. The situations they conjure up are quite different:

The road can be blocked by police ('and if we do this, we might intercept the criminals'–said by one detective to another).
The road may be blocked by flood water ('that possibly explains why our guests haven't arrived'–dialogue between husband and wife expecting visitors).

'Factual possibility' is stronger than 'theoretical possibility':

The pound can be devalued.
The pound may be devalued.

The second of these two statements is far more worrying (for those who are interested in the health of the sterling currency) than the first. It is not hard to see why this is: CAN *be devalued* merely postulates a theoretical possibility, a general idea in the mind; MAY *be devalued* actually envisages the event as a real contingency. The first sentence could be uttered at any time; the second only at a time of financial crisis.

a. It would be pleasant if the auxiliaries *can* and *may* corresponded exactly with the 'factual' and 'theoretical' types of possibility. But in reality, it seems possible (at least in formal English) to insert *may* in either of the contexts above, i.e. to use it for both 'factual' and 'theoretical' possibility. One may speculate that this, like the invasion of *can*'s territory by *may* in the sense of permission, (§§ 113A, 114B), is the result of hostility to *can* on the part of generations of pedagogues. It is interesting that with *can* and *may*, the linguistic law-givers seem to have succeeded in disrupting rather than enhancing the regularity of the language: they have destroyed, in formal English, the symmetry of *can* and *may* in relation to *have* and *must*. This symmetry persists, however, in colloquial English.

b. Can (= 'possibility') is typically found in general statements. Contrast *A friend can betray you*, an observation about friends in general, with *A friend may betray you*, which is more likely to be a warning about one particular friend.

122   The parallel difference between *must* (= 'factual necessity') and *have (got) to* (= 'theoretical necessity') is illustrated in these examples:

Someone must be telling lies
(= 'It's impossible that everyone is telling the truth').

Someone has (got) to be telling lies
(= 'It's impossible for everyone to be telling the truth').

Again the difference can be clarified by paraphrase—'factual necessity' being expressed by a *that*-clause, and 'theoretical necessity' by a *for*+ Noun Phrase+*to*+Infinitive construction. The 'factual'/'theoretical' distinction is less easy to seize upon here than in the case of *can* and *may*; but as 'theoretical necessity' means that the possibility of the opposite state of affairs cannot even be conceived of, *have (got) to* has a stronger force than *must*, and cannot be weakened, like *must*, to the meaning of 'logical assumption' (see § 115Ba). *Someone must be telling lies* voices a mere suspicion; *Someone has (got) to be telling lies* sounds more like an accusation.

Have (got) to (= 'necessity') is much less frequent (at least in BE) than *must* (= 'necessity'), however, because it is frequently unidiomatic. We tend to find another, roundabout way of expressing theoretical necessity:

These lines can't be by anyone but Shakespeare.
Nobody but Shakespeare could have written these lines.

Both of these negative alternatives come more naturally to the tongue than *These lines have to be by Shakespeare*.

'WILL'

123   In the last chapter (§§ 87–90), we considered the uses of *will* and *shall* as auxiliaries of future time; now it is time to look at them as modal auxiliaries. *Will* has four meanings under the second heading: WILLINGNESS, INSISTENCE, INTENTION and PREDICTABILITY.

A. WILLINGNESS ('WEAK VOLITION')

Who will lend me a cigarette? I will ('Who is willing . . .?). | My chauffeur will help you. | He'll do anything for money.

This meaning of *will* is common, especially in second-person requests: *Will you please open the door for me?* Weak-volitional *will* is normally unstressed, and can be abbreviated to *'ll*.

a. Will you . . .? in requests, although in logical terms a question about the listener's willingness, is in fact a politer substitute for an imperative. But there are even politer ways of making a request, and so *Will you . . .?* tends to sound peremptory unless toned down by further markers of politeness, including the use of the hypothetical Past Tense (see § 174): *Will you please . . .? Would you kindly . . .? Would you be good enough . . .?* One may compare another way of making a request by means of a volitional verb: *Would you like to open this door for me?*

B. INSISTENCE ('STRONG VOLITION')

He 'will go swimming in dangerous waters ('He insists on going swimming . . .'). | Janet, why 'will you keep making jokes about Aunt Betty? | I 'will go to the dance, and no one shall stop me!

This meaning of *will* is not very common, possibly because of the strong emotional overtones accompanying the idea of 'insistence'. With second- and third-person subjects, the feeling of exasperation at someone else's obstinacy is uppermost; with a first-person subject, the speaker makes his own uncompromising determination felt, with a force the verbal equivalent of banging one's fist on the table.

Strong-volitional *will* is always stressed, and cannot be contracted to *'ll*.

C. INTENTION ('INTERMEDIATE VOLITION')

I will write tomorrow. | We'll celebrate this very night! (= 'Let's!'). | We'll stop your pocket money if you don't behave.

Somewhere between the submissive volition of 'willingness' and the assertive volition of 'insistence' comes the intermediate concept of 'intention', illustrated in the above three examples. Occurring mainly with first person subjects, *will* in this sense conveys, according to context, a promise, a threat, or a corporate decision. The volitional element of meaning is reinforced by a feeling that in the act of speaking, a decision has been made, and that the fulfilment of the intention is guaranteed. There is thus a superimposition of predictive and volition-al meanings, which might have led to the inclusion of this use in Chapter 4 as a 'volitionally-coloured future'. (See, however, §§ 124C, 125, 127). This *will* is generally contracted to *'ll*.

All three volitional uses of *will* are limited to human or at least animate subjects; to say *My car 'will keep breaking down* is to suggest, by personification, that the car has a mind and will of its own.

D. PREDICTABILITY

By now he will be eating dinner. | That will be the milkman. | They will have arrived by now.

This third modal meaning of *will* is more closely related to the future meaning of *will/shall* (see §§ 87–90) than to the preceding volitional meanings. It is only a small step from the 'future prediction' associated with *will/shall* to the general idea of 'predictability' illustrated in the three sentences above. In *By now he will be eating dinner*, the speaker makes a 'forecast about the present' (in so far as such a thing is possible) concerning an event not directly observable. In the same way, some-one who hears the door-bell ring and exclaims *That will be the milkman* 'predicts' the identity of someone he cannot at that moment see.

To this extent, *will* (='predictability') belongs to contexts similar to those of *must* (='logical necessity'). In fact, *must* could replace *will* in all three examples above with only a slight change of effect.

The 'predictability' sense of *will* is naturally suited to scientific or quasi-scientific statements like *If litmus paper is dipped in acid, it will turn red*. Such conditional statements are of the general form: 'When-ever *x* happens, it is predictable that *y* happens'. They refer to a series of events, and therefore are the habitual (see § 13) equivalent of the examples given at the head of this section.

In many general statements, whether of a proverbial, scientific, or some other kind, habitual 'predictability' comes to have the force of 'typical or characteristic behaviour'. Thus:

A lion will attack a man only when hungry (='It is predictable or characteristic of lions that they attack men only when hungry')

Truth will out (='It is typical of truth that it makes itself known')

To *Truth will out* another proverb may be added: *Accidents will happen*, which means roughly 'It is a predictable or characteristic fact about accidents that they happen'.

'Characteristic behaviour' is also the meaning of *will* in descriptions such as:

He'll go all day without eating. | On racing days, he'll be in the betting-shop by ten o'clock, and there he'll stay till the pubs open. | She'll chatter away for hours on end if you give her a chance.

Will (='predictability') is normally without stress, and may be contracted to *'ll*.

a. In the proverb *Boys will be boys*, *will* may be given either a 'predictability' interpretation or a volitional interpretation. If *will* is unstressed, the meaning is: 'It is predictable or characteristic of boys that they behave like boys'. If *will* is stressed, the sense is 'strong volition', i.e.: 'Boys insist on behaving like boys'.

b. The choice of adverbial is often crucial for distinguishing the 'predictability' sense of *will* from the future 'prediction' sense. *He will have arrived by now* is 'predictability'; *He will have arrived tomorrow* is 'prediction'.

c. The use of *will* in general scientific statements suggests its comparability with the Simple Present in its 'unrestrictive' or 'habitual' senses (see §§ 8, 13). *Oil floats on water* and *Oil will float on water* are more or less equivalent statements. On the other hand, there are no 'predictability' statements equivalent to habitual statements like *Deciduous trees lose their leaves in autumn*; *The London train leaves at 4.20 daily*. This must be because the recurrent events described in these sentences are so utterly certain or pre-determined that to talk in terms of their predictability is to introduce a superfluous element of doubt. It would be a poor train service in which a departure time was 'typical' only. If the notion of 'prediction' (as suggested in § 87) involves the conceivability of error, perhaps the same applies to the related notion of 'predictability'.

d. There is a type of sentence in which *will* indicates 'disposition': *This watch won't work* (='I can't make this watch work'); *The auditorium will seat 500* (='One can seat 500 people in the auditorium'); *Will the window open?* (='Can one open the window?'). As the parentheses show, this use of *will* is closely connected with the 'possibility' sense of *can*; it can, however, be treated as a type of 'predictability' meaning, in which a conditional clause is understood: *The auditorium will seat 500 (if required)* etc.

'SHALL'

124 In statements with second- and third-person subjects, *shall* has two infrequent uses corresponding to those of *will* described in §§ 123A and 123B above; the difference, however, is that *shall* implicates the will of the speaker, rather than that of the subject of the sentence. With first-person subjects, it has a third meaning corresponding to that of § 123C.

A. WILLINGNESS ('WEAK VOLITION') ON THE PART OF THE SPEAKER

He shall be rewarded if he is patient. | Good dog, you shall have a bone when we get home (='I am willing for you to have a bone . . .'). | You shall stay with us as long as you like.

Shall so used is rare, especially amongst younger speakers of English. This is probably on account of the unpleasant connotation of condescension it bears. The implication is that THE SPEAKER IS CONFERRING A FAVOUR; consequently, one is unlikely to hear this use of *shall* except in address to pets or young children.

B. INSISTENCE ('STRONG VOLITION') ON THE PART OF THE SPEAKER

You 'shall obey my orders! ('I insist that you obey . . .'). | No one shall stop me. | He 'shall be mine!

This meaning is also of very restricted use, and carries strong overtones of imperiousness. Like the preceding use of *shall*, it is undemocratic, in suggesting that the listener's will is entirely subservient to that of the speaker. This may account for its obsolescence in present-day English, and the tendency to prefer *must* or the 'democratic imperative' *can* (see § 114C*b*). Outside fairy-stories (where it is frequently on the lips of ogres, wicked uncles, jealous stepmothers, etc.), this *shall* is even less likely to be encountered than that of 'weak volition'.

a. A similar use of *shall* with second- and third-person subjects for commands was formerly widespread, as is seen from the wording of the Ten Commandments in the Book of Common Prayer and the Authorized Version of the Bible: *Thou shalt not kill*, etc. Nowadays this archaic usage survives in legal and quasi-legal documents, such as rules for card games and academic dress: *A player who bids incorrectly shall forfeit fifty points*; *The hood shall be of scarlet cloth, with a silk lining of the colour of the faculty*.

C. INTENTION ('INTERMEDIATE VOLITION') ON THE PART OF THE SPEAKER

I shall write tomorrow. | We shall celebrate this very night! | We shall stop your pocket money if you don't behave.

Like *will*, *shall* has an intermediate volitional sense of 'intention', which does not, however, overlap with the preceding two volitional meanings, as it occurs exclusively with a first-person subject. As the examples make clear, *shall* becomes interchangeable with *will* (= 'intention') here, and such being the case, it may be wondered why these two uses are not included under *will/shall* in the 'predictive' sense of Chapter 4 (§§ 87–9), where again *will* and *shall* become interchangeable in the first person. The reason for treating them separately in this chapter will be shown when we study the relation between *will* and *shall* more carefully, particularly in questions (§§ 125, 127).

RELATION BETWEEN VOLITIONAL 'WILL' AND 'SHALL'

125 In modal as in future meanings, the interpretation of *shall* is limited according to the person of the subject: for positive statements, the rule is that with a first-person subject, *shall* indicates intention, but with a second- or third-person subject, it indicates 'strong' or 'weak' volition. The interpretation of *will*, on the other hand, is the same for all persons.

The volitional meanings of *will* and *shall* as so far discussed can be summarised:

WILL A. 'weak volition' of subject	B. 'strong volition' of subject	C. 'intermediate volition' of subject
SHALL A. 'weak volition' of speaker (2nd and 3rd person)	B. 'strong volition' of speaker (2nd and 3rd person)	C. 'intermediate volition' of speaker (1st person)

From this a consistent difference between *will* and *shall* is apparent: *will* signifies the subject's volition, while *shall* signifies the speaker's volition. When speaker and subject coincide, i.e. with first person subjects, *shall* and *will* (= 'intention') become interchangeable.

126 We have just been dealing with the vertical difference in the above table (that between *will* and *shall*), but there is something to be said about a horizontal difference, that between 'weak' and 'strong' volition. This relation is in fact in every way parallel to that between 'permission' and 'obligation' and that between 'possibility' and 'necessity'. In short, as we see from the following equivalence, 'willingness' is the INVERSE of 'insistence' (see § 118):

Some people 'will get in the way (= '. . . insist on . . .') = Not everyone will keep out of the way (= 'is willing to . . .').

Thus we may represent these two volitional meanings of *will* and *shall* by a diagram parallel to those of §§ 119 and 120:

	the volition of the subject		
	WILL	WILL	
Willingness ('weak')			Insistence ('strong')
	SHALL	SHALL	
	the volition of the speaker		

As in the other diagrams, the left–to–right contrast represents the relation of inverseness.

MODAL AUXILIARIES IN QUESTIONS

127 The rules for using modal auxiliary verbs in questions are sometimes different from those that apply to statements.

As already noted in §§ 113A*a* and 115A*a*, *may* and *must* in questions indicate THE LISTENER'S AUTHORITY rather than that of the speaker. In other words, when we ask questions we anticipate the attitude of the person being asked, and use the form appropriate for his reply:

May I open the window? ('Will *you* permit . . .?')
Yes, you may ('Yes, *I* do permit . . .')
Must they lock the door? ('Will *you* oblige . . .?')
Yes, they must ('Yes, *I* do oblige . . .')

Such a change of person is also found in questions with *shall*:

Shall I carry your suitcase? ('Do you want me to carry your suitcase?') | Shall we have dinner? ('Do you agree with my intention to have dinner?')

Questions beginning *Shall I* or *Shall we*, which are a normal way of offering help or an invitation to another person in English, obviously consult THE WILL OF THE LISTENER, not that of the speaker. However, in questions there is a slight additional modification of the meaning of *shall* in statements: the volitional meaning is a neutral one of 'wanting', rather than the weak sense of 'willingness' or the strong sense of 'insistence'. It is nearest to the intermediate meaning of 'intention', although it is slightly less forceful. The same meaning combines, though less often, with third-person subjects: *Shall Gwen do your shopping for you?* (spoken by a mother offering the services of her daughter to a neighbour).

If *shall* is followed by *you* (or *we* with the sense of 'you and I') it is the 'intention' meaning that is present, mirroring the occurrence of this meaning with the first person in statements: *Shall you take a holiday this summer?* (BE: 'Do you intend to . . .?'). Again, it is the listener's rather than the speaker's will that is questioned; and as in first-person statements, in second-person questions, *shall* and *will* (= 'intention' are interchangeable, although *shall* is probably much less common. This switch from first to second person makes it preferable to treat intentional *will* and *shall* as modal meanings belonging to this chapter, rather than future meanings belonging to Chapter 4.

The following tables summarise the volitional uses of *shall*:

VOLITIONAL 'SHALL'

STATEMENTS (speaker's volition)				QUESTIONS (listener's volition)		
	W	S	I		'WANT'	I
1st pers			*I/we shall*	1st pers	*shall I/we?*	*(shall we?)*★
2nd pers	*you shall*	*you 'shall*		2nd pers ·		*shall you?*
3rd pers	*he* etc *shall*	*he* etc *'shall*		3rd pers	*shall he* etc?	

(W= 'weak volition'; S= 'strong volition'; I= 'intermediate volition')
★Where *we* includes reference to the listener (='you and I/we')

It is worthwhile bearing in mind, however, that none of these uses, except perhaps those in the first person, are very common.

a. In AE, one may go further, and say that *shall*, whether in its future or volitional uses, is generally avoided by the use of an alternative construction; for example, *Should we go?* rather than *Shall we go?*

b. *If* clauses are in many ways like questions (e.g. in co-occurring with *any*, *anyone*, *ever*, etc. rather than *some*, *someone*, *sometimes*); it is therefore not strange to find auxiliary usage in *if* clauses following the rule for questions rather than the rule for statements. Examples from BE are the frequently heard tag of politeness *if I may* (e.g. *I'll have another biscuit, if I may*), which obviously means 'If you will permit me' rather than 'If I will permit myself'; and *if you must go*, which implies self-compulsion by the listener (cf. *I must go*).

128   *May* in its 'possibility' sense does not occur at all in questions, where its function is usurped by *can*. Notice, for example, that the question *Can they have missed the bus?* would precede a response *Yes, they may have done*, rather than *Yes, they can have done*. The distinction between 'factual' and 'theoretical' possibility therefore disappears in questions.

129   *Need* as an auxiliary verb may be considered the negative and interrogative counterpart of *must* in both the sense of 'compulsion' and that of 'logical necessity'. In questions, however, the semantic distinctions which obtain between *must* and *have* (*got*) *to* in statements seem to fade away, so *need* is virtually interchangeable with *Do . . . have to* or *Have . . . got to*:

{ Need I have a passport?	{ Yes, I'm afraid you must
{ Do I have to have a passport?	{ Yes, I'm afraid you have to

{ Need anyone be lying?	{ Yes, they must be
{ Does someone have to be lying?	{ Yes, they have to be.

a. This auxiliary verb *need* must be carefully distinguished from the full verb *need* occurring in the construction *need*+*to*+Infinitive (see § 143).

b. In AE, *do . . . have to* is the only question form in common use: *have I to . . .* and *need I . . .* are more or less restricted to BE, and *have I to . . .* is becoming infrequent even there.

c. A distinction is sometimes felt between *do . . . have to*, conveying a habitual or iterative meaning, and *have . . . got to* expressing a single present occasion. For example: *Do you have to be at work by 9 o'clock?* ('Is that what you have to do every day?'); but *Have you got to be at work by 9 o'clock?* ('Is that what you have to do this morning?').

130   *Must* occurs alongside *need* and *do . . . have to* in questions, but only in rather special circumstances, viz:

(1) to express obligation imposed by the listener (see § 127).

(2) in what one may call 'positively orientated' questions; that is, when the question form presupposes some positive assertion that has been mentioned in or suggested by the preceding conversation:

MR. X: Well, the purse isn't here, so we'd better look for it at the station.

MRS. X: *Must* it be at the station? We could have dropped it elsewhere, you know.

Here, *must* means something like 'Your attitude suggests that the purse must be at the station, but I am asking you to question that view'. The purpose of this interrogative type of *must* is to get the other person to reconsider his assumptions. It is often preceded by *why*: *But why must doctors be so much better treated than bus-drivers?*

131   *Must*, *need*, and *do . . . have to* are all used in a querulous type of question (usually with a second-person subject) already mentioned in §115A*a*:

Must you make that dreadful noise? | Do we have to have jam roll and custard every day? | Need you drop ash all over my best carpet?

Although the logical meaning of these auxiliaries is 'Is it . . . obligatory', the force of the question is probably ironic, communicating at two levels: 'Is it a fact that you can't help this annoying behaviour . . .? (but of course, I know very well that you *could* help it if you wanted to!)'.

a. The question form *have. . .got to*, incidentally, could not precisely replace *do. . .have to* above, as it would tend to suggest external rather than internal compulsion. *Have we got to have jam roll and custard every day?* is not an ironic question, but a simple inquiry 'Is there a regulation compelling us to have it every day?'

b. Again, one can compare a similar usage in *if* clauses: *If you must smoke . . .* , etc. (see §115A*a*).

THE MODAL AUXILIARIES AND NEGATION

132   If we examine the following pairs of sentences, we see that *not* can mean two very different things, according to which auxiliary verb it is combined with:

(a) ⎧ He can't be serious
⎪   ('It is *not* possible [that he is serious]')
(b) ⎨ He may not be serious
⎪   ('It is possible [that he is *not* serious]')
(c) ⎧ You don't have to go yet
⎪   ('It is *not* compulsory [for you to go yet]')
(d) ⎨ You mustn't go yet
⎩   ('It is compulsory [for you *not* to go yet]')

The meaning of each sentence containing a modal can, as we have seen, be broken down into the modal statement itself (the statement of possibility, necessity, etc.) and the statement on which the modal statement comments (that within square brackets above). Sometimes the insertion of *not* (or *n't*) after the modal auxiliary negates the modal statement (in examples (a) and (c) above, *not* falls outside the square brackets). In other cases (examples (b) and (d)), the other statement is negated. The first type of negation may be called EXTERNAL NEGATION (i.e. 'outside the brackets'), the second type INTERNAL NEGATION.

The following are examples of EXTERNAL NEGATION (the colloquial contracted forms *can't*, *needn't*, etc. are cited rather than the full forms):

May not (= 'permission'):
    You may not go
        ('I do not permit you [to go]')

Cannot, *can't* (all senses):
    You can't smoke here
        ('You are not permitted [to smoke here]')
    You can't be serious
        ('It is not possible [that you are serious]')
    He can't drive a car
        ('He is not able [to drive a car]')

Doesn't/don't have to, *haven't* (*got*) *to* (both senses):
    You don't have to pay that fine
        ('You're not obliged [to pay that fine]')
    It doesn't always have to be my fault
        ('It is not necessary [for it to be always my fault]')

G

Need not, needn't
>   You needn't pay that fine
>> ('You are not obliged to pay that fine')
>   It needn't always be my fault
>> ('It is not necessary [for it to be always my fault]')

Examples of INTERNAL NEGATION are:

May not (='possibility')
>   They may not come if it's wet
>> ('It is possible [that they won't come if it's wet]')

Must not, mustn't (='obligation')
>   You mustn't keep us all waiting
>> ('I oblige you [not to keep us all waiting]')

Will not, won't (in all senses)
>   Don't worry—I won't interfere
>> ('I'm willing [not to interfere]')
>   He won't do what he's told
>> ('He insists on [not doing what he's told]')
>   They won't have received my letter yet
>> ('It is predictable [that they haven't received my letter yet]')

Shall not, shan't (='strong' and 'weak' volition)
>   Don't worry—you shan't lose your reward
>> (roughly 'I'm willing to see [that you don't lose your reward]')
>   You shan't escape my revenge!
>> (roughly 'I insist on seeing [that you don't escape my revenge]')

There is normally no negation of *must* in the sense of 'necessity'.

Won't in the strong-volitional sense of 'refusal' is more common than the corresponding sense of *will*.

There is no logical difference between external and internal negation with *shall* (='intention'): *I shan't go if it rains* means 'I do not intend to go' or 'I intend not to go'.

a. When the meaning of *may not* is 'permission', the stress normally falls on *not*; when the meaning is 'possibility', the stress normally falls on *may*. Thus: *You may 'not disturb us* (='You are not permitted to disturb us') contrasts with *You 'may not disturb us* (='It is possible that you will not disturb us'). The rare (obsolescent?) British contraction *mayn't* applies in the sense of 'permission' only.

b. In AE, *may not* is less used in the sense of 'possibility'. It can be replaced by other expressions, such as *might nots* (§ 175).

c. The contraction *shan't* is not found in AE.

d. An occasional case of 'double negation' is observed with modal auxiliaries, especially with *can*: *I can't not tell her about it*. In such cases, internal and external negation are combined in the same clause. The meaning is 'It is impossible for me *not* to tell her about it'.

133 A number of differences between positive and negative interpretations of the modals need to be noted.

Because *can* and *may*, *have got to* and *must* are not generally comparable in their negative and question forms, the 'factual'/'theoretical' contrast which exists in positive statements is not discernible in negative statements or questions. On the other hand, *may not* and *mustn't* keep the implication of the speaker's authority in contrast to *cannot* and *don't have to*. *You may not* means 'I do not allow you . . .' and *You mustn't* means 'I forbid you . . .'.

Shan't (= 'strong volition') is used even with first-person subjects, so that *I shan't!* (the cry of a disobedient child) is synonymous with *I won't*.

134 The type of meaning-contrast earlier called 'inverseness' (see §§ 118, 126) leads to a curious equivalence, in the negative, of auxiliaries which in a positive context have opposite meanings:

You may not smoke in here (= 'I don't permit you to smoke . . .')
You mustn't smoke in here (= 'I oblige you not to smoke . . .')

Both these statements are prohibitions, and only differ in that the second sounds perhaps more forceful, positively forbidding instead of negatively refusing permission. The secret of this equivalence is that the 'inverse' opposition of the two meanings is cancelled out by the contrast between external and internal negation. There is a rough equivalence, for the same reason, between *There doesn't have to be an answer to every question* and *There may not be an answer to every question*.

a. The fact that a different type of negation neutralises inverseness of meaning makes it difficult to decide whether *won't* and *shan't* in their 'strong' and 'weak' volitional senses are instances of internal or external negation. One can paraphrase the 'refusal' meaning in *He won't do what he's told* either by 'He insists on not doing what he's told' or by 'He is not willing to do what he's told', the difference between the two being merely a matter of emphasis. How, then, does one choose between the two explanations? In this case, phonology provides the answer: the uncontracted form *will not* in this context demands a stressed *will* (see § 123B), so we are justified in associating

won't in the 'refusal' sense with 'strong volition'. There is contrary phono-
logical evidence for treating the other sense of *won't* as 'weak volition'
('willing . . . not' rather than 'not insist'): this is the possibility of replacing
won't by the contracted form *'ll* (see § 123A) followed by *not*: *Don't worry,*
I won't interfere=*Don't worry, I'll not interfere.* There are no comparable
grounds for treating *shan't* in the same way, but since in volitional interpretations *shall* is in other respects parallel to *will*, we are perhaps justified in
assuming external negation here as well, for lack of evidence in the other
direction.

MODAL AUXILIARIES IN RELATION TO TENSE AND ASPECT

135   FUTURE TIME. None of the modal verbs we have been considering has a special construction for future time, except *have to*, which
combines with *will/shall* and *be going to*, (and shows, by that fact, that
it is not, syntactically speaking, an auxiliary verb):

We'll have to meet next week.

This is to be contrasted with:

We must meet next week
We may meet next week
We can meet next week

where the true auxiliary verbs are unchanged for the expression of
future time. The forms *may, can, must*, etc. might, indeed, best be
called Non-past rather than Present Tense, as they neutralise the contrast between present and future time.

When an 'event verb' (see § 12) is combined with an auxiliary, we
generally assume that the event referred to is in the future, even when
there is no time adverbial to point in that direction: *May we come too?*
You must give me all the information you have; *They can wait their turn.*

a. There is also, however, the possibility of interpreting an 'event verb' as
'habitual present': *She can cook very well.* This may well be the more common
interpretation with *can* (='ability') and *will* (='predictability').

136   PAST TIME. To express past time, most modals have special Past
Tense forms:

PRESENT		PAST	PRESENT		PAST
may	~	*might*	*need*	~	—

can	~	could		will	~	would
must	~	—		shall	~	should

The two exceptions, as we see from the above list, are *must* and *need*, both of which have no Past Tense counterpart (on the Past Tense form *needed to*, see § 143).

The following are examples of Past Tense forms used in reference to past time in direct speech (indirect speech will be separately considered in Chapter 6, § 151):

May (='permission') (unusual, chiefly BE)
 The prisoners might leave camp when they wished

Can (='permission')
 The prisoners could leave camp when they wished

Can (='possibility')
 In those days, a transatlantic voyage could be dangerous

Can (='ability')
 Few of the tourists could speak French

Have to (='obligation')
 Children had to behave themselves when I was a lad

Have to (='logical necessity')
 Someone had to be the loser

Will (='willingness')
 He would risk anything for gain or adventure

Will (='insistence')
 The annoying thing was that he 'would leave the house in a muddle

Will (='predictability')
 In Spring the birds would return to their nests.

a. *Would* (='predictability') is more commonly used than *will* (='predictability'), being popular in historical or fictional descriptions of character, typical behaviour, etc.: *In his last years, the King would spend whole days in morose solitude, speaking only to his immediate family and refusing all official audiences. At such times he would behave with the utmost churlishness to his ministers, and would fly into a violent rage whenever his will was crossed.*

b. The rules of stress for *will* apply also to *would*: with the strong–volitional meaning, it has to be stressed; otherwise it is generally unstressed, and may be contracted to *'d*.

c. The usual Past Tense of *have* (*got*) *to* is *had to*; *had got to* (BE) is limited to indirect speech: *I told him he'd got to hurry up.*

d. Could and *might* have 'state' meaning, while the roundabout expressions *was permitted/allowed to, was able to,* etc. denote events, and add an implication of 'fulfilment' to the ordinary meaning of the modal auxiliary. *We were able to reach camp that night* conveys the message 'We were able to, and moreover we did'; in a similar fashion, *We were permitted to leave camp early* suggests the extra information that we actually *did* leave camp early.

137   MEANINGS NOT AVAILABLE WITH THE PAST TENSE. Gaps are left in the expression of past modality not only by the absence of Past Tense forms for *must* and *need,* but by the non-occurrence of certain meanings of *might* and *should. Might* is not used in senses B. and C. ('possibility', 'benediction and malediction'; see § 113) and *should* is not used in any of the volitional senses (it is, however, used as the Past Tense of *shall* in indirect speech, and in hypothetical clauses).

Even in the 'permission' sense, *might* in direct speech is sufficiently rare to be discounted. We may therefore present a simplified picture of past modal meaning as follows: for all intents and purposes, neither *may* nor *must* have Past Tense equivalents, and their special nuances of meaning ('speaker's authority' and 'factual possibility/necessity') can therefore not be expressed in the Past. Instead, *could* and *had to* are the natural Past Tense translations of *may* and *must*:

Visitors may ascend the tower for sixpence this summer→
   Visitors could ascend the tower for sixpence last summer.

I must confess his latest novels bore me→
   I had to confess his latest novels bored me.

138   PERFECT ASPECT. The Perfect Infinitive following a modal auxiliary assigns past time to the meaning of the main verb, as distinct from the meaning of the auxiliary itself. There is thus a difference between *In those days voyages could be dangerous*, which informs us of a PAST POSSIBILITY (see § 136), and *The voyage may have been dangerous*, which informs us of the (PRESENT) POSSIBILITY of a PAST DANGER. It may be a little misleading, though, to talk of 'present possibility', as a possibility tends to be a timeless thing, akin to the 'eternal truth' of scientific and proverbial statements (see § 8). It is for this reason that expression of past possibility by means of *could* is rather unusual.

In its infinitive form, the Perfect Aspect (see § 67) is a general marker of past time, without respect to the 'definiteness' and 'indefiniteness' which distinguish Past Tense and Present Perfect with finite verbs. Thus it covers the area of meaning which, in finite verbs, is divided between Perfect and Past (see § 64). Note the use of different tenses in these two paraphrases of *may have come*:

> They may have come already
> (= 'It's possible that they *have come* already')

> They may have come last year
> (= 'It's possible that they *came* last year').

The Perfect Infinitive can be combined with temporal adverbs which could not occur with the Present Perfect of finite verbs: one could not say ★ *They have come last year*.

139 PERFECT AND PROGRESSIVE ASPECTS. The Perfect and Progressive Aspects are ordinarily incompatible with the meanings of 'ability', 'permission' and 'obligation', and also with the volitional meanings of *will* and *shall*. It makes no sense, for instance, to give someone present permission to do something in the past: *You may have seen me yesterday* (as opposed to *You may see me tomorrow*) necessarily has the meaning of 'possibility', not 'permission'.

The remaining meanings, those available with the Perfect and Progressive Aspects, are exemplified below:

May (= 'possibility')
> You may have left your wallet on the bus
> He may be bluffing

Can (= 'possibility')
> Can you have made a mistake? (BE)
> He can't be working at this hour!

Must (= 'necessity')
> You must have left your wallet on the bus
> I must be dreaming

Have to (= 'necessity')
> He has to have passed Advanced Level in two subjects before he goes to University
> To speak excellent English, you don't have to be living in England

Will (= 'predictability')
> They will have read your letter by now
> Don't phone him yet – he will still be eating his breakfast.

a. Can is rarely used with the Perfect outside questions (in BE) and negative statements.

OTHER VERBAL CONSTRUCTIONS EXPRESSING 'CONSTRAINT'

140   Something must finally be said about five other verbs and verb constructions which have meanings in some ways similar to *must* and *have to*. Of these, *ought to*, *should*, and *(had) better* qualify at least marginally as auxiliary verbs, whereas *need to* and *am/is/are to* are more like full finite-verb constructions.

141   OUGHT TO has the same meaning as *must*, except that it expresses not confidence, but rather lack of full confidence, in the fulfilment of the happening described by the main verb. For example, if one says *You must buy some new shoes*, one assumes that the purchase will be carried out: the tone of *must* tolerates little argument. But *You ought to buy some new shoes* is a different matter—the speaker here could well add under his breath 'but I don't know whether you will or not'. *Ought to* is a less categorical equivalent of *must* both in its sense of 'obligation' and its sense of 'logical necessity' (see § 115):

'OBLIGATION BY SPEAKER'

He must pay for the broken window
('. . . and moreover he *will* do so, because I say so')

He ought to pay for the broken window
('. . . but he probably won't')

'LOGICAL NECESSITY'

Our guests must be home by now
('I conclude that they are, in that they left half-an-hour ago, have a fast car, and live only a few miles away')

Our guests ought to be home by now
('I conclude that they are, in that . . . , but whether my conclusion is right or not I don't know—perhaps they were hindered by some unforeseen occurrence such as a breakdown').

Ought to weakens the force of *must* (= 'logical necessity') by indicating that the speaker has doubts about the soundness of his conclusion. An optimistic treasure-seeker would say, after working out the position by the aid of maps, *This is where the treasure must be*; a more cautious one would say *This is where the treasure ought to be*, so acknowledging that there might well be something wrong with his assumptions or his calculations. This sense of *ought to* can often be equated with 'high probability'.

142   SHOULD can be used as an alternative to *ought to* in both senses:

He ought to pay for the broken window=
  He should pay for the broken window

Our guests ought to be home by now=
  Our guests should be home by now.

Ought to is normally stressed, whereas *should* is normally unstressed. This use of *should* has no counterpart in *shall*.

a. The negative forms *oughtn't to* and *shouldn't*, parallel to *mustn't* (see § 132), are further instances of internal negation. *One oughtn't to complain* is a weakening of *One mustn't complain*, carrying the supposition '. . . but perhaps one does'. Unlike *mustn't*, however, *oughtn't to* and *shouldn't* can bear the second interpretation 'logical necessity'; as such, they represent a weakening of the meaning of *cannot* (='impossibility'). (This is because *mustn't* as the internal negation of 'necessity', if it existed, would be equivalent to *can't* as the external negation of 'possibility' – see § 132–4.) Hence *You oughtn't to have any difficulty getting the tickets* means approximately 'If my calculations are correct, you can't possibly have any difficulty getting the tickets'; or in effect, 'It is unlikely that you will have any difficulty'. (The contracted form *oughtn't to* is seldom found in AE)

b. *Ought to have* and *should have* with reference to past time have a stronger negative connotation of 'contrary to fact'; *She should have seen my car coming* has the presupposition '. . . but in fact she didn't'.

143   NEED TO. In the construction *need* + *to* + Infinitive, *need* is a full or 'lexical' verb forming question and negative forms with *do* (*Does he need to . . . ? We didn't need to . . .* ; etc.), and taking Present and Past Tense endings (*He needs to rest*; *He needed to rest*; etc.). It is therefore not to be grammatically confused with the auxiliary verb *need* (§ 129), despite a similarity of meaning. Since *need* as an auxiliary is practically confined to questions and negative statements, it is only the *need to* construction that can be used in ordinary positive statements.

In terms of meaning, *need to* is half way between *must* and *ought to*: it asserts obligation or necessity, but without either the certainty that attaches to *must* or the doubt that attaches to *ought to*:

SCALE OF INTENSITY

(1) You must get a hair-cut (most categorical)

(2) You need to get a hair-cut

(3) You ought to get a hair-cut (least categorical)

Yet there is a difference in the quality, as well as in the degree of constraint. For *must* and *ought to*, the constraint or obligation comes from outside rather than inside (except for *I/we must* – see § 115). If I say *You must get a hair-cut*, I am exerting my own authority over the person addressed; but if I say *You need to get a hair-cut*, I am primarily pointing out to the 'you' in question the constraint that his own situation imposes upon him: viz. that his hair is too long, that he looks untidy, and that it is for his own sake that a hair-cut is to be recommended. One can make a similar comparison of *He ought to feel wanted* and *He needs to feel wanted*: the one expresses an external and the other an internal compulsion.

It is useful to note that in this construction, the main verb *need* has the same meaning as when it is followed by a direct object. The following sentences are virtually synonymous:

My boots need to be cleaned = My boots need a clean.
He needs to practise more = He needs more practice.

The auxiliary verb *need* and the main verb *need* + *to* scarcely differ in effect on many occasions:

{ Need you wake him up?
{ Do you need to wake him up?

But in other contexts one can draw a clear distinction between them. Let us suppose that Lady P. addresses her gardener with the words: *The hedges needn't be trimmed this week, Smithers*. This means 'You are excused the task – I shall not oblige you to trim the hedges this week' (perhaps because Lady P. is feeling kind, or because she has more important jobs in mind for Smithers). But the import is quite otherwise if she says: *The hedges don't need to be trimmed this week, Smithers*. The point she makes here is that the hedges do not require attention – because, we presume, they have not grown enough to make them look untidy.

144   AM/IS/ARE TO. This construction, consisting of a finite form of the verb *to be* followed by *to* + Infinitive, is similar in meaning *to have (got) to* and *ought to*; in fact, it can frequently be substituted for either of these modal forms. Its main difference from *have (got) to* is that its principal meaning includes the specific idea of 'ordering' or 'commanding':

He is to return to Germany tomorrow
> (The most likely meaning here is 'He has received explicit orders to return to Germany')

He has to return to Germany tomorrow
> (This could suggest he has received orders, but more likely it means 'Circumstances oblige him to return' – e.g. he has run out of money, he has an appointment in Germany, his ticket expires tomorrow, etc.)

Occasionally *am/is/are to* is used in a quasi-imperative way by the person actually giving the orders: *You and the others are to report back to me at dawn tomorrow*. It is significant that the word *please* could be added to this sentence, just as if it were a grammatical command.

In other contexts, *am/is/are to* loses its imperative flavour, and becomes a way of indicating a future happening already determined (by plan, decree, or arrangement) in the present:

> They're to be married in St. James's church, and Jill's to be bridesmaid. | The meeting is to take place in Oxford.

The verbal construction here declares that the decree has been laid down, or the plan made, by someone other than the subject of the sentence. Often, the suggestion is that it is part of an official programme. Otherwise, the meaning is very close indeed to those of the Present Progressive and Simple Present in a future sense (§§ 97–104):

> The Minister is to meet union officials tomorrow
> The Minister is meeting union officials tomorrow
> The Minister meets union officials tomorrow.

These three sentences are almost indistinguishable in meaning. If, however, the final adverb were deleted, only the first would retain its future meaning; that is, although the Present Progressive and Simple Present Tenses can signify 'future plan or arrangement', they normally only have that interpretation when accompanied by a future adverbial. The usefulness of the *am/is/are to* construction partly lies in its ability to signify future meaning even when no specific future time is mentioned: *The Queen is to have a holiday*.

Syntactically, *am/is/are to* is like an auxiliary verb to the extent that it has no non-finite forms. One cannot say, for example, ★ *The meeting may be to take place at Oxford*, as one can say *The meeting may have to take place at Oxford*.

The Past Tense forms *was/were to* can normally only express the imperative sense of *am/is/are to* in indirect speech: *They told me I was to collect the papers the next day. Was/were to* commonly express 'plan or programme', however (*The meeting was to take place at Oxford the next day*); and in addition, they have a pure future-in-the-past meaning 'was/were destined to': *Thirty years later, this precocious youth was to be the first President of the United States* (see § 84).

a. Am/is/are to with the interpretation 'Plan for the future' is characteristic of newspaper reports, and in headlines, the construction is abbreviated to *to* + Infinitive through the ellipsis of the form of the verb *to be*: UNESCO CHIEF TO VISIT AFRICA; MISS UNITED KINGDOM TO MARRY FILM BOSS.

b. A special use of *am/is/are to* in *if* clauses adds to the notion of 'condition' that of 'purpose': *If we are to win the competition, we must start training now.* The meaning of the *if* clause here is close to 'In order to win the competition . . .', or 'If we are going to (i.e. intend to) win the competition . . .'.

c. There is another idiomatic use of *am/is/are to* with the verb *come* (or, in elevated literary style, with the verb *to be*): *The best is still to come; The best is yet to be.* Both of these could be paraphrased 'The best is still ahead of us, in the future'. They can be compared with a similar construction with *have: I have yet to see him smile.* However, in all three cases, the infinitive is a complement rather than part of the finite-verb construction.

d. Was/were to can be employed in *if* clauses as a marker of hypothetical meaning (see § 166).

145 (HAD) BETTER. This construction, often abbreviated in familiar colloquial English to *better*, is like *ought to*, in that although it is Past Tense historically and in outward form, in present-day English it has no Present Tense equivalent, and in meaning is 'present' rather than 'past'.

(*Had*) *better* is not so categorical in its coercive import as *must*; it signifies exhortation or strong recommendation rather than compulsion:

You'd better be quick (roughly='I urge you to be quick').
He better not make a mistake (roughly='I warn him not to make a mistake').

Past time or past-in-the-future time may be indicated, in very familiar speech, by the Perfect Infinitive: *You'd better have changed your mind when I call tomorrow.* A construction with the Progressive is also possible: *You'd better be working harder than this when the boss comes back.*

Six

Indirect Speech

146   The distinction between DIRECT SPEECH and INDIRECT SPEECH (or reported speech) is demonstrated in these two sentences:

(A) DIRECT SPEECH   (B) INDIRECT SPEECH

I enjoy playing cricket → Jim said that he enjoyed playing cricket

Sentence (A) specifies the words actually uttered by Jim, while sentence (B) reports the fact that he uttered them. Sentence (B) is more or less equivalent to: (C) *Jim said 'I enjoy playing cricket.'*

a. Actually, there is a slight difference between sentences (B) and (C): whereas (A) indicates the actual words spoken by Jim, (B) only reports the *meaning* of sentence (A). Thus (B) could be a report of a sentence *I like playing cricket* which is synonymous, but not identical to (A).

BACK-SHIFT

147   If the verb in the main or REPORTING CLAUSE is in the Past Tense, it is usual for a verb in the reported clause to be BACK-SHIFTED:

'I loathe cricket'→John said that he loathed cricket.
'He's being a fool'→Everyone thought he was being a fool.
'You've deceived me'→I told her she had deceived me.
'Did you see the accused on the night of the 25th?'→
She was asked whether she had seen the accused on the night of the 25th.

There are two possible types of back-shift: Present→Past (including Present Perfect→Past Perfect) and Past→Past Perfect. The second type is illustrated in the last example above.

In semantic terms, back-shift may be explained quite simply as follows. The time of the original speech, which is 'now' for direct speech, becomes 'then' for indirect speech, and all times referred to in the speech accordingly become shifted with respect to that point of orientation:

SPEECH ABOUT	'now' (Pres. T.)	→ PAST REPORT OF SPEECH ABOUT . . . (Past T.)	'then' (Past. T.)
SPEECH ABOUT	'then' (Pres. Perf. or Past)	→ PAST REPORT OF SPEECH ABOUT . . . (Past T.)	'before then' (Past Perf.)

a. If the utterance in direct speech contains a verb in the Past Perfect, no back-shift is possible, as English has no means of expressing 'before-before-then' by tense or aspect: *'Max had already gone when I phoned him this morning'* → *Jim said that Max had already gone when he (had) phoned him that morning.*

148 Although back-shift is the rule when the reporting verb is in the Past Tense, the speaker can sometimes, if he wishes, BREAK THE CONCORD between reporting verb and reported verb, keeping the tense form of the original speech:

'I loathe cricket'→John confessed that he *loathes* cricket.

'The police are still looking for him'→We were told the police *are* still looking for him.

'No one has ever spoken to me'→She complained that no one *has* ever spoken to her.

The implication of this avoidance of back-shift is that the time of the original utterance ('then') and the time of the report are both included within the time-span indicated by the verb of the reported clause. The circumstances in which this is the case are best illustrated by historical statements:

55974

'Virtue is knowledge' → Socrates said that virtue was knowledge
                OR   Socrates said that virtue is knowledge.
'I am blameless' → Socrates said that he *was* blameless
    BUT NOT ★ Socrates said that he *is* blameless.

The obvious difference between these cases is that the statement *Virtue is knowledge* is of eternal application, and can therefore have reference to the present day (the time of report) as well as to the time of Socrates; but the declaration *I am blameless*, as spoken by Socrates, has no reference to the present time, since Socrates is now dead.

Speeches expressing 'general truths' (e.g. of a proverbial or scientific nature) are, for this reason, likely to keep to the Present Tense even in indirect speech. In general, the back-shift rule can be ignored with 'unrestrictive' (§ 7) and 'habitual' (§ 13) uses of the Simple Present, while with the 'instantaneous present' (§ 9) it has to be obeyed. *Napier passes the ball to Attwater* could not, say, be turned into indirect speech as ★ *The commentator said that Napier passes the ball to Attwater.*

a. When the Past Tense has a global indefinite meaning in combination with *ever, always,* etc. (see § 64*d*), back-shift is compulsory: *I always said he was a liar* (NOT ★*I always said he is a liar*).

b. There is an interesting parallel between back-shift of tense and the shift from first- and second-person to third-person pronouns in cases like *I enjoy cricket → He says* HE *enjoys cricket.* Just as the 'concord' of tenses may be broken in special circumstances, so the third-person rule may be broken in cases where people mentioned in the reported clause are identical with participants in the reporting situation. For example *'You're a fraud, Sam' → He told me I was a fraud* (spoken by Sam).

c. The back-shift from Simple Past or Present Perfect to Past Perfect may also be waived: *I once met President Kennedy* can be rendered in indirect speech as either *She said she had once met President Kennedy* or *She said she once met President Kennedy.*

149   The back-shift rule applies not just to indirect speech in the strict sense, but also to REPORTED FEELINGS AND THOUGHTS. In fact, it applies more regularly with verbs such as *know, think, realise, forget,* than with verbs such as *say* and *tell*:

> I forgot you were listening (rather than 'I forgot you are listening'). |
> I didn't know he was a teetotaller (rather than 'I didn't know he is a teetotaller').

In these cases one can scarcely substitute the Present Tense, even though the verb would normally be applicable to the time of reporting. On the other hand, one could say *I realised that life is a gamble* as well as . . . *was a gamble*.

AUXILIARY VERBS AND INDIRECT SPEECH

150 For purposes of back-shift, a modal auxiliary followed by a Perfect Infinitive can IN REPORTING CLAUSES, as in other contexts, be counted as the equivalent of a Past Tense form:

'What is wrong?' → You *ought to have asked* the mechanic what was wrong.

'They are bluffing' → You *must have realised* that they were bluffing.

'I'm guilty' → He *may have admitted* he was guilty.

If we paraphrase this last example 'It is possible that he admitted he was guilty', we use the Past Tense *admitted*, and show that in terms of meaning, this is no exception to the back-shift rule.

151 IN REPORTED CLAUSES, the back-shifting of an auxiliary results in the use of the Past Tense form *would, should, might*, etc. Whereas these Past Tense forms are not always usable in direct speech (e.g. *It might rain* is not the direct Past Tense equivalent of *It may rain* – see § 137), in indirect speech they apply without exception:

'Visitors may ascend the tower for sixpence' → The brochure declared that visitors might ascend the tower for sixpence.

'It may rain' → We were afraid it might rain.

'You can help me carry the cases' → He said that we could help him carry the cases.

'You shall have an ice-cream when we get home' → They promised that he should have an ice-cream when he got home.

'Shall I open the window?' → He wondered whether he should open the window.

'You will keep interrupting me' → He complained that I would keep interrupting him.

'The plan will fail' → I warned them that the plan would fail.

The last example shows the back-shift of future *will* to a 'reported past future' *would*. This *would* is many times more common than the direct future-in-the-past *would* described in § 84. The back-shift of future *shall* to *should* is also possible alongside *would* with a first-person subject: *I told them that we would/should lose the battle unless they tried harder.*

a. Volitional *should* is acceptable following verbs such as *promised, decided, insisted,* and *intended,* even where the corresponding direct speech use of *shall* would be unusual and rather declamatory: *He promised we should have our reward*; *We decided that the house should be built of stone.*

152 *Must, ought to, need* and *(had) better* have no Past Tense forms (see §§ 136, 141, 145), but in indirect speech they may themselves be used as if they were Past Tense forms. That is, *must* is back-shifted to *must*, *ought to* to *ought to*, etc.:

'You must reach camp by ten' → They were told they must reach camp by ten.

'You ought to be ashamed of yourself' → He told me I ought to be ashamed of myself.

'You'd better hurry up' → He warned her she'd better hurry up.

153 The auxiliaries *may, must, shall,* and *ought to* (as we have seen in §§ 113A, 115A, 124, and 141) involve the speaker as the person who exerts his will or authority. In indirect speech, the same principle holds good, both for these auxiliaries and their back-shifted variants *might* and *should,* so long as we remember that it is THE SPEAKER OF THE REPORTED SPEECH whose will or authority is in question. A sentence like *John has told her she may stay,* in other words, is a true translation into indirect speech of *John has told her 'You may stay'*: if *may, must,* etc. are applicable in direct speech, they are also applicable in indirect speech. Ordinarily the speaker of the reported speech is also the subject of the main or reporting clause:

Jenkins says you must pay before you go
Jenkins says they ought to be ashamed of themselves
Jenkins promised we should have our reward.

In each of these cases it is Jenkins (subject of the main clause) whose authority or will is invoked by the modal auxiliary.

a. Notice that the normal restriction of volitional *shall* to second- and third-person subjects (§ 124) does not apply in indirect speech: *He has promised we shall have our reward,* with the first-person subject *we,* is an indirect-speech version of *You shall have your reward.*

H

FREE INDIRECT SPEECH

154   FREE INDIRECT SPEECH, a very common device of narrative writing, consists in reporting an utterance indirectly by back-shifting the verb whilst omitting (or parenthesising) the reporting clauses (*He said* . . ., etc.) which are the conventional signals of indirect speech.
DIRECT SPEECH: *Agnes:* 'Why do they always have to pick on me?'
INDIRECT SPEECH: Agnes asked why they always had to pick on her.
FREE INDIRECT SPEECH: Why did they always (groaned Agnes) have to pick on her?

or simply: Why did they always have to pick on her?

The convention of free indirect speech is a more flexible medium for reporting than normal indirect speech; it also aids concision by allowing a writer to retell someone's words indirectly and at length without having to keep inserting expressions like *He said* or *She exclaimed*.

Free indirect speech, unlike ordinary indirect speech, can incorporate the question and exclamation structures of direct speech:

> Could he be imagining things? (wondered Harry) | Here was Bagby at last! (thought John) | How many years had he and his sister dreamed of this moment! | So that was their plan, was it!

It can also, as these sentences show, include words such as *here* and *this*, which are generally replaced by *there* and *that* in indirect speech proper.

The use of free indirect speech for describing 'interior monologue' has become a very widespread, if not standard practice in the fiction of the twentieth century. Instead of *He said* . . . we have to imagine an omitted reporting clause such as *He thought* . . ., *He said to himself* . . ., *He reflected* . . .:

> Once or twice on the way to the station, once or twice as the train stopped on the route to Paddington, William was tempted to give up the expedition in despair. Why *should* he commit himself to this abominable city merely to be railed at and, for all he *knew* of Lord Copper's temperament, physically assaulted? But sterner counsels prevailed. He *might* bluff it out. Lord Copper *was* a townsman, a provincial townsman at that, and certainly *did* not know the difference between a badger and a great crested grebe.
>
> (Evelyn Waugh, *Scoop*, Ch. II, 2)

The Past Tense verbs in italics in this passage are clearly in indirect speech; they narrate the train of thought in William's mind, and represent a soliloquy that could be otherwise represented in direct speech as 'Why should I commit myself to this abominable city . . .' etc.

Next to direct question and exclamation forms, the clearest (sometimes the only) indicators of free indirect speech are back-shifted verbs in the Past Tense. For example, *would* in main clauses often invites construal as the back-shifted equivalent of future *will*, none of the other senses of *will* (volitional, conditional, direct future-in-the-past) being suitable to the context: *That evening he would be seeing Sylvia again.*

Seven

Theoretical and Hypothetical Meaning

155   The contrast between the Subjunctive and Indicative Moods has largely disappeared from present-day English grammar, but the distinction of meaning which the Subjunctive and Indicative used to express is still important within the language. In fact, modern English has a threefold distinction between FACTUAL, THEORETICAL, and HYPOTHETICAL meaning.

THE SUBJUNCTIVE MOOD

156   Such as it is, the Subjunctive survives, in modern English, in both Present Tense and Past Tense forms.

The PRESENT SUBJUNCTIVE appears to be used more in AE than in BE, where it is little more than an archaism of legalistic style:

It is proposed that the Assembly *elect* a new Committee. | If an Association member *be* found guilty of misconduct, his membership shall be suspended and appropriate dues refunded.

Subjunctive Mood is here shown by the absence of *-s* from the third-person singular Present Tense verb, and by the use of *be* in place of the Indicative *am/is/are*. (Notice the legalistic use of *shall* in the second example – cf. § 124B*a*.) Whether it occurs in conditional, concessive, or noun clauses, the Present Subjunctive is an indicator of non-factual or THEORETICAL meaning (see §§ 157–8).

The Past Subjunctive, on the other hand, expresses HYPOTHETICAL MEANING. It survives as a distinct form from the Indicative only in the use of *were*, the Past Tense form of the copula, in the singular as well as in the plural: *If he* WERE *my friend, he would speak for my cause.* Although this form is of more widespread occurrence than the Present Subjunctive *be*, it is nowadays frequently, if not usually, replaced by the Past Indicative *was*: *If he was my friend . . .*

a. The Subjunctive singular *were*, however, still prevails in formal style, and in the familiar phrase *If I were you . . .*

b. In addition to its occurrence in subordinate clauses, the Present Subjunctive lives on in set exclamatory wishes such as *God be praised! Long live anarchy! Lord have mercy upon us! Heaven help them!* But here again there is a more common alternative construction, the construction with *may* mentioned in § 113C: *May God be praised!* etc.

THEORETICAL MEANING

157   The contrast between factual and theoretical meaning was introduced in §§ 120–22, where it was pointed out that as auxiliaries of possibility and necessity, *may* and *must* are 'factual', whereas *can* and *have (got) to* are 'theoretical'. It was noted, by way of exemplification, that while *The pound can be devalued* (= 'It is possible for the pound to be devalued') treats devaluation as an IDEA, *The pound may be devalued* ('It is possible that the pound will be devalued') treats devaluation as a possible FACT, and to that extent has a stronger and more threatening meaning.

The factual/theoretical contrast is by no means confined to the area of possibility and necessity, as further examples show:

$$\begin{cases} \text{(a) It's a pity (for Bill) to refuse such an offer (IDEA)} \\ \text{(b) It's a pity that Bill refused such an offer (FACT)} \end{cases}$$

$$\begin{cases} \text{(c) It's nice to be young (IDEA)} \\ \text{(d) It's nice being young (FACT)} \end{cases}$$

Firstly, it may be noticed that the theoretical examples (a) and (c) contain infinitive constructions, where the factual sentences (b) and (d) contain a *that*-clause and a gerund construction.

Secondly, with regard to meaning, it may be noted that the factual sentences imply the truth of the statements they contain, whereas the theoretical sentences do not. Thus sentence (b) lets us know that Bill *did in fact* refuse the offer; sentence (*a*) does not tell us whether he did or not. The factual sentence, we may say, is TRUTH-COMMITTED, whereas the theoretical sentence is TRUTH-NEUTRAL (that is, leaves the question of truth and falsehood open).

158   The above observations about sentences (a)–(d) cannot, unfortunately, be generalised to apply to all cases of factual and theoretical meaning. They are useful clues, not infallible tests.

The most one can do, with regard to grammatical form, is to give the following list of constructions *normally* expressing one meaning rather than another:

FACTUAL MEANING: Indicative mood in dependent clauses
                   Gerund construction

THEORETICAL MEANING: *to* + Infinitive construction
                       should + Infinitive in dependent clauses
                       Present Subjunctive

All these constructions are illustrated now with the same introductory phrase *It's a good thing*:

FACTUAL MEANING:

It's a good thing that he recognizes his faults
Him recognizing his faults is a good thing (OR LESS COLLOQUIALLY: His recognizing his faults is a good thing)

THEORETICAL MEANING:

It's a good thing for him to recognize his faults
It's a good thing that he should recognize his faults
It's a good thing that he recognize his faults (rare, archaic)

But these correlations should not be pressed too far. After some verbs of reporting, for example, the *to* + Infinitive construction is factual:

I know him to be an imposter = I know he is an imposter

Furthermore, whether a sentence is truth-neutral or truth-committed often depends on factors other than the choice of verbal construction. In *I'm surprised that your wife should object*, the effect of the main verb is to cancel out the neutrality of the *should*+Infinitive construction, with the result that we clearly understand from this sentence that the wife does object. There is hence no logical difference, in many cases, between *should*+Infinitive and the simple Indicative form *objects*. This is not to say, however, that there is no difference in feeling: in *I'm surprised that your wife should object*, it is the 'very idea of it' that surprises me; in *I'm surprised that your wife objects*, I am surprised by the objection itself, which I take to be a known 'fact'.

The meaning changes in the opposite direction (from truth-commitment to truth-neutrality) through the influence of verbs such as *believe* and *suppose*:

I believe that his mother is dead. | I suppose you're waiting for my autograph.

Because of the essential element of uncertainty in the meanings of these verbs, a *that*-clause that would elsewhere be truth-committed becomes truth-neutral. The same applies to adjectives like *possible* and *likely*.

a. In support of the distinction drawn here between factual *that*-clauses and theoretical ones (with *should*), observe the different choice of construction in these sentences: *This fact—that man destroys his environment—worries us deeply; This idea—that man should destroy his environment—worries us deeply*. It would not be possible here to change the positions of the nouns *idea* and *fact*.

b. Similarly, note that of the following four sentences, the fourth is unacceptable: *I like to see you; I'd like to see you; I like seeing you; *I'd like seeing you*. This is because the strong element of doubt in the hypothetical construction *I'd like* (§§ 163–4) conflicts with the truth-commitment of the gerund construction *seeing you*.

c. As one would expect from the above discussion, *that*-clauses with the Subjunctive may be converted into *that*-clauses with *should* without any change of meaning: *The Law-Lords have decided/decreed/insisted/voted that the existing law (should) be maintained*. In this sense, the *should*+Infinitive construction might be called, historically speaking, a 'subjunctive substitute'. Note, however, that the *should* construction is usable in many *that*-clauses where the Subjunctive is impossible: *It is interesting that the play should be a huge success*. The Subjunctive appears to be restricted to *that*-clauses expressing some element of wish or intention.

d. Should as a 'subjunctive substitute' ought to be carefully distinguished from *should*='ought to'; and yet in many instances it is difficult to tell from context which meaning is meant to apply. Does one interpret *They agree that the rules should be changed* as 'They agree that the rules be changed' or 'They agree that the rules ought to be changed'? In practice, there is little difference between these interpretations.

e. There are a number of idiomatic uses of theoretical *should* in exclamations and questions: e.g. *That he should think me capable of it!* (='the very idea!'); *We were having a great time, when who should come along but Skinflint Kemp* (='Who do you imagine came along . . .?')

f. May/might+Infinitive, like *should*+Infinitive, may be regarded as a 'subjunctive substitute' in a few contexts: *Let us fight on, though the world may be against us* (='though the world be against us'); *Let us fight on, in order that future generations may bless our memory* (='. . . that future generations bless our memory'). Nowadays this usage is confined to an elevated literary style, and it is in any case generally possible to assign to *may* one of its more common meanings of 'permission' or 'possibility' in such utterances.

CONDITIONAL SENTENCES

159 In CONDITIONAL SENTENCES, the proposition expressed by the main clause is qualified by a condition expressed by an *if*-clause or some equivalent construction (e.g. a clause introduced by *unless*, *lest*, or *whether*). Conditional sentences can express either a REAL CONDITION ('open condition') or an UNREAL CONDITION:

> If you touch me, I'll scream (REAL CONDITION)
> If you touched me, I'd scream (UNREAL CONDITION).

We may start by discussing real conditions.

160 In REAL CONDITIONS, both the main clause and the dependent clause are truth-neutral: hearing the remark *If he proposes to me, I'll marry him*, we are not in a position to judge whether either the proposal or the marriage will take place. Nevertheless, it is normal, in contemporary English, to use the factual Indicative form of the verb in both clauses. (For future conditions, the Simple Present is used rather than *will*+Infinitive in the dependent clause–see § 101.) Although the most common type of real condition, as in the above example, refers to the future, there are no special restrictions on the time reference of conditions, or on the tense forms used to express them. The following examples illustrate something of the variety and mixture of times and tense forms permitted:

> If you're happy, you make others happy
> (Simple Present+Simple Present)
> If John told you that last night, he was lying
> (Simple Past +Simple Past)

If my son is a genius, I've underestimated him
(Simple Present + Present Perfect)

If they left at nine, they will certainly be home by midnight
(Simple Past + *will* 'future').

161   The truth-neutrality of an *if*-clause is reflected in the possibility of using constructions expressing theoretical meaning (Present Subjunctive and *should* + Infinitive) in place of the Simple Present:

PRESENT SUBJUNCTIVE: If the server *serve* a fault twice, he shall lose a point (archaic, legalistic).

should + INFINITIVE: If you *should hear* news of them, please let me know.

The effect of the theoretical *should* is to make the condition slightly more tentative and 'academic' than it would be with the ordinary Present Tense.

a. A more formal expression of a tentative real condition is achieved by omitting *if* and inverting the subject and auxiliary *should*: *Should you change your mind, there will still be a place open for you.*

162   UNREAL CONDITIONS are normally formed by the use of the Past Tense (Indicative or Subjunctive) in the conditional clause, and *would* + Infinitive in the main clause. Thus it is possible to derive unreal conditions from the examples of real conditions in § 160 by a process of 'back-shift' similar to that employed in indirect speech:

If you were happy, you would make others happy. | If John had told you that last night, he would have been lying. | If my son were a genius, I'd have underestimated him. | If they had left at nine, they would certainly be home by midnight.

The precise grammatical and semantic nature of this switch from real to unreal conditions is discussed in the following account of hypothetical meaning (especially §§ 166–7).

HYPOTHETICAL MEANING

163   When a verbal construction expresses HYPOTHETICAL MEANING, this implies an assumption, by the speaker, that the happening described did not, does not, or will not take place. For example, if someone says *I wish I* WAS *beautiful and clever*, he implies '. . . but I am *not* beautiful and clever'; if he says *Just suppose I hadn't applied for the job*, the suggestion is '. . . but I *have* applied for the job'. In effect, this implication is considerably weakened in some contexts (see §§ 168*a–c*, 173); but it is this NEGATIVE TRUTH-COMMITMENT of hypothetical meaning that distinguishes it both from factual (positive truth-commitment) and from theoretical (truth-neutrality) meaning.

The difference between the three meanings is registered in a simple way, in the three sentences:

Factual:
It's laughable that Septimus is in love ('Yes, it's a fact that he is in love').

Theoretical:
It's laughable that Septimus should be in love ('Whether he *is* in love or not is a different matter').

Hypothetical:
It would be laughable if Septimus were in love ('But actually, he's *not* in love').

Of the three attitudes to Septimus' being in love, the first and the third are contrary, while the second is on neutral territory between them.

a. The negative feeling of the hypothetical construction is demonstrated by the rough equivalence of *I wish she loved me* (hypothetical) and *It's a shame she doesn't love me* (negative factual).

164   Apart from unreal conditions such as *If you were happy, you'd make others happy* (§ 162), hypothetical meaning is found IN DEPENDENT CLAUSES in a number of less important sentence-types:

It's time you were in bed ('. . . but you're not').
He behaves *as if* he owned the place ('. . . but he doesn't')
It's not *as though* we were poor ('. . . we are not')
Suppose/imagine you and I were to find ourselves on a desert island (. . . but I assume we won't).
If only I had listened to my English teacher! ('. . . but I didn't').
Even though he were my brother, I would cast him out ('. . . but he is not') (archaic).
I wish I were young again ('. . . but I'm not').
I'd rather you listened to me.

Of these constructions, those with *it's time*, *if only*, and *wish* require hypothetical verb forms, while those with *as if*, *as though*, *suppose/*

imagine, even though and *would rather* permit a choice between hypo-thetical and non-hypothetical forms. The difference between the second sentence above and *He behaves as if he owns the place* is that the sentence with *owns* leaves the question of whether he owns the place open, whereas the sentence with *owned* presupposes that he does not. (However, context may suggest a negative presupposition also in the first sentence.)

165 IN MAIN CLAUSES, a hypothetical verb form normally requires the presence of an accompanying conditional clause. *★ The Eiffel Tower would fall down* on its own is not a self-sufficient English sentence, because unless we add a condition to it, the listener is left baffled, consciously or unconsciously asking the question 'If what?'. There are however, various special circumstances in which a hypothetical main clause may stand on its own, and one can often explain such cases by positing a SUPPRESSED CONDITION. For example:

(1) I'd be inclined to trade that car in for a new one (*suppressed condition:* '. . . if I were you').

(2) Would you like some peas? ('. . . if I offered you some').

(3) No, I'd prefer/I'd rather have beans, please ('. . . if you wouldn't mind').

(4) I'd hate to live in a house like that ('. . . if I had to').

(5) Would you let me have a match? ('. . . if I were to be so bold as to ask you for one').

As examples (2)–(4) show, we commonly make use of a suppressed hypothetical condition in expressing a desire. Apparently this is because there is a certain indelicacy in expressing one's wishes bluntly, a statement of wish often being interpreted as an imperative. *I'd like beans* is therefore more polite than *I want beans*. It removes from reality the whole question of whether I am going to get beans or not, or rather, makes the diplomatic assumption that I am *not* going to receive any.

The most important cases of suppressed conditions involve the modal auxiliaries, and will be dealt with later in §§ 172–5.

a. The evasive use of hypothetical forms in sentences like *It would seem there has been a mistake*; *One would suppose the danger is over*; *I would hope that the balance of payments will improve next year* is difficult to explain in terms of a suppressed condition. In each case, the non-hypothetical form could be used instead, and it seems that the function of the hypothetical form here is simply to indicate the speaker's reluctance to commit himself on matters of personal feeling or judgement. This usage is something of an affectation in discursive, academic styles of English; e.g. in radio discussion programmes.

b. The idiomatic construction *would rather/sooner* (='would prefer') is an instance of a hypothetical verb form without a non-hypothetical equivalent.

166   The GRAMMATICAL MARKERS of hypothetical meaning are:

1 *Would/should*+Infinitive
   (a) in main clauses;
   (b) in reported speech clauses which would be main clauses if converted into direct speech;
   (c) but not in any clause (main or dependent) containing a modal auxiliary, as modals have no Infinitive form.

2 Past Tense (Indicative or Subjunctive)
   (a) in other dependent clauses;
   (b) in any clause containing a modal auxiliary.

3 The Past Tense construction *was/were to*+Infinitive (Indicative) or *were to*+Infinitive (Subjunctive) as an alternative to the plain Past Tense
   (a) in conditional clauses;
   (b) in clauses following *suppose/imagine*;
   (c) only in reference to future time.

Examples:

(1a) I *would love* to live abroad (if I had the money).

(1b) She claims that she *would love* to live abroad.

(1c) *If I could drive a car, I *would can* teach you.

(2a) He talks as if he *was/were* my rich uncle.

(2b) If I could drive a car, I *could teach* you.

(3a) If you *were to learn* Spanish, you might get a better job.

(3b) Just suppose that crocodile *were to escape*!

(3c) *If you *were to know* Spanish, you might get a better job.

Where the Past Tense or *would/should*+Infinitive is used to signal hypothetical meaning, pastness of time can be conveyed by the Perfect Aspect. The hypothetical version of the past real condition *If she called yesterday I was out* is therefore *If she had called yesterday, I would have been out*.

a. In literary English, a conditional clause with inversion of subject and auxiliary verb is sometimes used instead of an *if*-clause: *Had I known* (='If I had known'); *Were he to return* (='If he were to return . . .'); *Were they alive* (='If they were alive . . .'). *Had* and *were* are the auxiliaries most commonly involved. *Was* is rarely preposed because in the rather elevated style in which this inversion occurs, the Subjunctive is preferred to the Indicative form. Inversion is just possible with *could* and *might*, but not with *would*: *Could/might I but see my child once more* (='If only I could/might see my child once more . . .'). Here the inversion, which has a decidedly archaic, rhetorical flavour, has to be supported by the intensificatory word *but*. Comparison may be made between such inversions and the similar inversion of *should* in real-conditional sentences (§ 161*a*). It should be noted, incidentally, that *should* is sometimes used as if it were a marker of unreal conditions, rather than of tentative real conditions: *Should the container explode, there would almost certainly be widespread damage.*

b. Sentences such as *I wish it would rain* appear to be exceptions to the rule that in dependent clauses, hypothetical meaning is conveyed by the Past Tense rather than *would/should*+Infinitive. In fact they are not exceptions, since *it would rain* in this context is the hypothetical equivalent of future *it will rain* rather than of present *it rains*. Hence the difference between *I wish this clock worked* and *I wish this clock would work* is that the former is a wish about the present, and the latter a wish about the future. In practice this means (since events are more easily placed in the future rather than at the present moment–cf. § 135) that we use the future *would* for 'event verbs', and the present hypothetical Past Tense for 'state verbs' (e.g. we would not say *★I wish that book would belong to me*, but we might say *I wish someone would buy me that book*). *Would* in this position often has volitional colouring: *I wish you wouldn't joke about my moustache!* Such remarks often have the force of indirect commands.

167 The following tables plot past, present, and future time against real and unreal conditional sentences, (1), (2) and (3) being the three grammatical markers of hypothetical meaning listed in § 166:

	PAST TIME	PRESENT TIME	FUTURE TIME
REAL	Past Tense Pres. Perf. Tense Past Perf. Tense	non-perf. Pres. Tense	*will/shall*+Infin. etc. non-perf. Pres. Tense

	PAST TIME	PRESENT TIME	FUTURE TIME
UNREAL	(1) *would/should* +Perf. Infin. (2) Past Perf. Tense (3) *was/were to*+ Perf. Infin.	(1) *would/should* +Infin. (2) non-perf. Past Tense	(1) *would/should* +Infin. etc. (2) non-perf. Past Tense (3) *was/were to*+ non-perf. Infin.

It is evident from this table that there is little difference, in unreal conditions, between the expression of present and of future time. This means that a sentence like *If you were happy, you'd make others happy* refers indifferently to the present or the future. We could insert either a future or a present adverbial to make the time-span explicit:

If you were happy to-day, you'd make others happy.
If you were happy next week, you'd make others happy.

(It is of incidental interest that there is no conflict, here, in the co-occurrence of a Past Tense verb with a future adverbial.) It might be appropriate with hypothetical, as with modal verb forms (see § 135), to call the tenses Past and Non-past, rather than Past and Present.

168   It is now time to think further about THE MEANING OF HYPO-THETICAL CONSTRUCTIONS.

It was established earlier that the distinguishing mark of hypothetical meaning is its implication of NEGATIVE TRUTH-COMMITMENT. The exact interpretation, however, varies in accordance with past, present, and future time.

In referring to imaginary past events, the hypothetical forms normally have the categorical sense of 'CONTRARY TO FACT', since it is not difficult to have definite knowledge of past events:

If your father had caught us, he would have been furious ('. . . but in fact he didn't').
What if we'd lost our way! ('. . . but in fact we didn't').
I wish I hadn't swallowed that last glass of whisky ('. . . but in fact I did').

Non-past imaginary happenings do not usually have such uncompromising implications. In the present, the sense is not so much 'contrary to fact' as 'CONTRARY TO ASSUMPTION'; in the future, it is weakened further to 'CONTRARY TO EXPECTATION':

> If you really loved me, you'd buy me everything I want ('. . . but I assume that you do not love me').
> If it snowed tomorrow, the match would have to be cancelled ('. . . but I don't expect it will snow').

The latter sentence does not rule out the possibility of snow, but on the other hand it is more optimistic in sentiment than the real condition *If it snows tomorrow, the match will have to be cancelled.*

a. The negative truth-commitment of hypothetical meaning is additionally weakened in sentences which suggest a course of action, such as *If we phoned the Berkinshaws we might get invited to dinner*, where the effect of the unreal condition is to emphasise the tentativeness of the suggestion, rather than to rule out its being put into force.

b. For a similar reason, hypothetical utterances which indirectly recommend a course of action to another (e.g. *I wish you'd go*) do not have the full value of 'contrary to expectation'; it is tact, rather than lack of hope, that leads the speaker to use a hypothetical form in such cases.

c. Yet a further example of weakening is seen in a colloquial tendency to use the *it's time* construction in circumstances to which the implication of negative truth-commitment is quite inappropriate. One might hear, for example, the following snatch of dialogue: A: *Tiny's cooking the breakfast this morning.* B: *Oh good—it's about time he helped out with the cooking.* It is quite evident that here the hypothetical verb *helped* refers to what Tiny is doing, rather than what he is not doing. If the hypothetical form is to be given any negative force here, it must be applied to the past (Tiny's previous failure to help) rather than to the present.

HYPOTHETICAL USE OF MODAL AUXILIARIES

169 Modals, it has been noted, have no infinitive form, and therefore cannot combine with *would* according to the normal rule (rule 1a, § 166) for expressing hypothetical meaning in main clauses. Instead, in main as in dependent clauses, THE HYPOTHETICAL MEANING OF A MODAL IS INDICATED BY THE PAST TENSE ALONE:

> If you could drive, you could teach me ('If you were able to drive, you would be able to teach me')

Notice that here the first *could* is replaceable by *were able to*, the second with *would be able to*.

a. Have (got) to, being a modal auxiliary only for purposes of meaning, has the infinitive form *have to*, and so in main clauses can combine with *would* to form the regular hypothetical form *would have to*.

170   Further difficulties arise because of gaps in the Past Tense paradigm of modal auxiliaries.

First, here are straightforward examples of unreal conditions expressed by means of the hypothetical Past Tense:

Might: If you loved me, I *might* marry you (= '. . . it's possible that I would marry you').

Could: If the astronauts momentarily lost radio contact with earth, the whole mission *could* be ruined (= '. . . it would be possible for . . .').

If you got a job in London, you *could* come to see us more often (= '. . . you would be able to. . .').

Would: If you were a gentleman, you'*d* do anything I asked (= '. . . you would be willing to . . .').

Against these must be placed the following gaps and exceptions:

1 *Might* and *could* rarely occur in unreal conditions with the sense of hypothetical permission.

2 The hypothetical forms of *will* (= 'strong volition', 'predictability') and *shall* (= 'strong volition', 'weak volition') appear to be non-existent.

3 As *must* has no Past Tense form, *would have to* is the only verbal expression available for hypothetical obligation or necessity:

  REAL CONDITION: If you're right, we *must* act at once.
  UNREAL CONDITION: If you were right, we'*d have to* act at once.

a. From the first two examples above, it will be seen that there is a difference of meaning between *might* and *could* as hypothetical auxiliaries of possibility. *Might* (= 'it is possible that . . . would') ascribes unreality to that which is possible; while *could* (= 'it would be possible for . . .') ascribes unreality to the possibility itself. This difference is analogous to that between internal and external negation.

b. Could in the 'ability' sense does not occur in a hypothetical main clause when the main verb is a 'state verb', referring to a permanent accomplishment: *If you'd had proper lessons, you could speak English.* Instead, *would be able to* or *would know how to* can be used.

c. There is a possible occurrence of the hypothetical form of strong-volitional *will* in exclamations like *You* WOULD *make a mess of it! He* WOULD *interfere!* But this idiomatic usage might equally be traced to the ordinary Past Tense use of *would* in direct speech.

171 With modal auxiliaries, past hypothetical meaning can be expressed by the Perfect Infinitive:

If you'd loved me, I *might have married* you. | Had you come to me sooner, I *could have cured* you. | If you'd asked him politely, he *would have mended* the cooker.

Would have had to is used for past hypothetical necessity or obligation: *If the police had caught us, we'd have had to make a clean breast of it.*

172 We turn finally to SPECIAL HYPOTHETICAL USES OF MODAL AUXILIARIES in main clauses where there is no expressed condition. The three main areas of meaning concerned are permission, volition, and possibility. These special uses can best be explained in terms of psychological factors such as diffidence and tact. Hypothetical forms are substituted in order to tone down the meaning of the non-hypothetical auxiliary where it might be thought too bold or blunt.

173 HYPOTHETICAL PERMISSION. *Could* and *might* are often used as more polite alternatives to *can* and *may* in first-person requests:

Could I see your driving licence? | Might I ask you for your opinion? | I wonder if we could borrow some tea?

The strict force of the hypothetical form here is that the speaker does not expect his plea to be granted, the negative inference being '. . . but I don't suppose I may'. It need scarcely be added that in practice, this is a further instance of weakening of hypothetical meaning, and that people will choose *could* and *might* out of a habit of politeness, even when they expect their requests to be complied with. If one should want to supply a 'suppressed condition' here, it might be '. . . if I were bold enough to ask you'.

a. This polite use is not altogether parallel with the 'permission' use of *can* and *may*, in that it is difficult to discern any special overtone of 'speaker's/ listener's permission' in the choice of *might* rather than *could* (see § 119). On

I

the other hand, *might* does parallel *may* in being more formal and polite than *could*.

b. One of the many ways of making a polite request in English is by the phrase *I don't suppose* followed by a clause containing hypothetical *could*. In this case, the negative presupposition of the hypothetical form is made explicit.

174   HYPOTHETICAL VOLITION. The polite use of *would* instead of *will* (='willingness') in second- and third-person requests furnishes a further example of the absolute use of a hypothetical clause with verbs expressing desire:

> Would you lend me fifty pence? | I wonder if someone would help me pitch this tent.

One may account for the air of politeness of these requests by postulating again some such unexpressed condition as '. . . if I were bold enough to ask you'. Compared with a direct imperative, the *will* question is itself, of course, a step in the direction of politeness (for it issues a directive in the form of a question rather than a command). But through habit, it has acquired strong imperative overtones, especially when delivered in a tone of command: *Will you sit down!* It is therefore not surprising that a still more indirect form of imperative, with hypothetical *would*, should have come into use.

a. This *would* (the hypothetical form of weak-volitional *will*) is to be carefully distinguished from *would* used purely as a marker of hypothetical meaning in main clauses. The former differs from the latter in that (a) it can be replaced by *will*; and (b) it can be paraphrased by *would be willing to*.

b. Significantly, the typical answer to a hypothetical request entails using the corresponding non-hypothetical auxiliary: *Would you lend me sixpence? Certainly I will* (likewise *Might I ask your opinion? Certainly you may/can*). The answerer is under no social pressure to be tactful in speaking of his own will.

175   HYPOTHETICAL POSSIBILITY. The hypothetical forms *could* and *might* are frequent as substitutes for *can* and *may* in expressing possibility:

> There could be trouble at the Springboks match tomorrow. | The door might be locked already. | Our team might still win the race.

The effect of the hypothetical auxiliary, with its implication 'contrary to expectation', is to make the expression of possibility more tentative and guarded. *Our team might still win the race* could be paraphrased 'It is barely possible that . . .' or 'It is possible, though unlikely, that . . .'.

A possible event in the past can be described by means of the construction *could/might* + Perfect Infinitive: *Could you have left your umbrella at the bus-station? I might have (done)*. In this respect, *could/might have* is a slightly more tentative variant of *can/may have* (see § 138).

It is difficult to see any difference in the use of *could* and *might* here, except that in the negative, *couldn't* is an instance of external negation, and *mightn't* an instance of internal negation:

He couldn't have made that mistake!
(= 'It is not even barely possible that he made that mistake')
He mightn't have made that mistake
(= 'It is just possible that he did not make that mistake').

In this contrast, *couldn't* and *mightn't* are parallel to *can't* and *may not* respectively. On the other hand, *might* (= 'possibility'), unlike *may* (= 'possibility'), can be used in questions: *Might I have left it at the bus-station?*

a. Both *could* and *might* are commonly used in suggestions for future action, in a way analogous to *can* (see § 114C*b*): *You could answer these letters for me; We might meet again after Christmas, if you're agreeable*. The set phrase *might as well* is sometimes used here instead of *might*. Predictably, the hypothetical forms *could* and *might* are more polite, in their directive force, than *can*, since they make the expression of possibility more tentative. Once again, the contrast between *can* and *may* seems to be smoothed away in the hypothetical forms: there is little to choose between *could* and *might* here, although in the non-hypothetical 'democratic imperative', only *can* is possible.

b. In familiar speech, *could* and *might* are used more forcefully, in a tone of rebuke, in such remarks as *You 'could try and be a bit more civilized! You 'might stop grumbling at me for a change!* The negative hypothetical implication is clearly present here: 'It would be possible for you to do these things, but you don't in fact do them'. Notice also the use of *could/might have* in complaints about past omissions: *You might have let me know the boss was in a foul temper! You could have given me some notice!*

176 In conclusion, it is worth noticing that there are three distinct interpretations of hypothetical *might* + Perfect Infinitive, all involving possibility:

You might have told me! (§175*b*)

   ('It would have been possible for you to tell me')

You might have dropped it somewhere (§ 175)

   ('It is barely possible that you (have) dropped it somewhere')

You might have met him if you'd been there (§ 171)

   ('It is possible that you would have met him . . .').

In the first two of these examples, it would be possible to replace *might* by *could* without any appreciable change of meaning. In the third, however, *could* would convey the somewhat different meaning 'It would have been possible for you to meet him if you'd been there'.

Guide to Further Reading

Allen, R. L., *The Verb System of Present-day American English*. The Hague, 1966. (Scholarly and thorough, although the grammatical apparatus is difficult; an excellent bibliography and detailed verb-lists)

Allen, W. Stannard, *Living English Structure*. London, 1955. (In this popular course-book, there is much valuable guidance on verbal meaning)

Behre, F., *Meditative-Polemic* SHOULD *in Modern English* THAT-*Clauses* (= Gothenburg Studies in English, 4). Stockholm, 1955.

Bodelsen, C. A., 'The Expanded Tenses in Modern English: An Attempt at an Explanation', *Englische Studien*, 71 (1936), 220–38.

Bolinger, D. L., 'More on the Present Tense in English', *Language*, 23 (1947), 434–6.

Boyd, J. and Thorne, J. P., 'The Semantics of Modal Verbs', *Journal of Linguistics*, 5 (1969), 57–74. (A recent interpretation of the English modals in terms of the philosophical notion of 'illocutionary force').

Bryan, W. F., 'The Preterite and the Perfect Tense in Present-Day English', *Journal of English and Germanic Philology*, 35 (1936), 363–82.

Bull, W. E., *Time, Tense and the Verb* (= University of California Publications in Linguistics, 19). Berkeley and Los Angeles, 1960. (A work of interest and originality, involving a comparison of time-tense relationships in a number of languages, including English).

Charleston, B. M., 'A Reconsideration of the Problem of Time, Tense, and Aspect in Modern English', *English Studies*, 36 (1955), 263–78.

Close, R. A., 'Concerning the Present Tense', *English Language Teaching*, 13 (1959), 57–66.

Close, R. A., *English as a Foreign Language*. London, 1962. (The subject of this book is much narrower than its title suggests: it is a perceptive study of problems of grammatical meaning in modern English, much attention being given to tense and aspect; well illustrated by diagrams).

Crystal, D., 'Specification and English Tenses', *Journal of Linguistics*, 2 (1966), 1–34. (A systematic investigation of the relation between choice of verb forms and of adverbials).

Curme, G. O., *Syntax* (= Vol. 3 of Curme, G. O., and Kurath, H.,

A Grammar of the English Language). Boston, 1931. (Chief American representative of the 'orthodox grammatical tradition'–see under Jespersen, MEG).

Dietrich, G., *Erweiterte Form Präteritum und Perfektum im Englischen*. München, 1955.

Diver, W., 'The Chronological System of the English Verb', *Word*, 19 (1963), 141–81. (This and the following article are somewhat procrustean attempts to systematise the semantics of tense, aspect, and modality in modern English).

Diver, W., 'The Modal System of the English Verb', *Word*, 20 (1964), 322–52.

Ehrman, M., *The Meanings of the Modals in Present-Day American English*. The Hague, 1966. (Based on a corpus of American English texts, this monograph is the most important study of the meanings of the modals to date. The approach (making use of the notions of basic meaning and subsidiary 'overtones') is, however, different from the present one, and frequently leads to different results).

Erades, P. A., 'Points of Modern English Syntax', *English Studies*, 38 (1957), 283. (On *can* and *may* as auxiliaries of possibility).

Gruber, S., 'Look and See', *Language*, 43 (1967), 937–47.

Hatcher, A. Granville, 'The Use of the Progressive Form in English: a New Approach', *Language*, 27 (1951), 254–80. (A classic article on the subject).

Hill, A. A., *Introduction to Linguistic Structures*. New York, 1958. (Pages 205–16 are devoted to the semantics of the verb phrase).

Hornby, A. S., 'Non-conclusive Verbs: Some Notes on the Progressive Tenses', *English Language Teaching*, 3 (1949), 172–7.

Huddleston, R., Review Article on M. Ehrman, *The Meanings of the Modals in Present-Day American English*, *Lingua* 23, 2 (1969), 165–76. (A good critique of Miss Ehrman's book, with many fresh and penetrating observations on the use of the modals).

Jespersen, O., 'Negation in English and Other Languages', reprinted in *Selected Writings of Otto Jespersen*, London and Tokyo, 1962, 3–151.

Jespersen, O., *A Modern English Grammar on Historical Principles* (MEG), Part IV. London and Copenhagen, 1931. (The best and best-known of 'traditional' reference grammars of English based on textual examples. Unsurpassed in the collection, classification, and discussion of copious examples, it suffers, from the viewpoint of the learner of contemporary English, from the general drawback of works of this genre: failure to separate present-day usage clearly from the now obsolete or obsolescent usage illustrated in writers of the past).

Jespersen, O., *Essentials of English Grammar*. London, 1933.

Joos, M., *The English Verb: Form and Meaning*. Madison and Milwaukee, 1964. (A bizarre book, full of confusions and over-simplifications, yet also full of insights. It makes use of a British English corpus).

Koziol, H., 'Das emphatische Praesens-pro-Futuro im Englischen', *Englische Studien*, 68 (1933), 81–6.

Kruisinga, E., *A Handbook of Present-Day English*. Part II: *English Accidence and Syntax*. Groningen, 1931. (This and the following volume are numbered among the orthodox 'reference grammars' mentioned under Jespersen, *MEG*).

Kruisinga, E., and Erades, P. A., *An English Grammar*. 2 Vols. 8th edition. Groningen, 1953–60.

Lebrun, Y., CAN *and* MAY *in Present-Day English*. Brussels, 1965. (After a study of texts, Lebrun concludes–contrary to the view presented in this book–that the differences between uses of *can* and *may* are mainly a matter of style).

Leech, G. N., *Towards a Semantic Description of English*. London, 1969. (A book concerned with problems both of theory and of description; it contains two chapters on 'time' and 'modality' in which some of the material of this book is treated on a more theoretical level).

Leisi, E., 'Die Progressive Form im Englischen', *Neueren Sprachen*, 9 (1960), 217–26.

Manning, C. A., 'English Tenses and Slavic Aspects', *Slavistica*, No. 34 (1959).

McIntosh, A., 'Predictive Statements', in *In Memory of J. R. Firth*, ed. C. E. Bazell et. al., London, 1966, 303–20.

Millington-Ward, J., *The Use of Tenses in English*. London, 1954.

Osman, N., *Modern English*. London, 1964.

Ota, A., *Tense and Aspect of Present-day American English*. Tokyo, 1963.

Palmer, F. R., *A Linguistic Study of the English Verb*. London, 1965. (Combines grammatical and semantic study; detailed, sound, and not too theoretical).

Palmer, H. E., and Blandford, F. G., *A Grammar of Spoken English*. 3rd edition, revised and rewritten by R. Kingdon. Cambridge, 1969.

Poutsma, H., *A Grammar of Late Modern English*. 5 Vols. Groningen, 1904–16. (See comment on 'traditional' reference grammars under Jespersen, *MEG*).

Schopf, A., *Untersuchungen zur Wechselbeziehung zwischen Grammatik und Lexik im Englischen*. Berlin, 1969. (Chapters 2 and 3 on Aspect).

Storms, G., 'That-clauses in Modern English', *English Studies*, 47 (1966), 249–70.

Sweet, H. (1892), *A New English Grammar, Logical and Historical*. Vol. I. Oxford, 1892.

Twaddell, W. F., *The English Verbal Auxiliaries*. Providence, R. I. 1960. (A short tract giving a neat and concise statement of forms and their attendant meanings in the English verb phrase. The brevity of the treatment inevitably brings some over-simplification).

Zandvoort, R. W., *A Handbook of English Grammar*. 5th edition. Longman, 1969. (The most up-to-date, and certainly the most popular, of the 'traditional' reference grammars – see comment under Jespersen, *MEG*. Chapters 4–6 deal with verbal constructions and their meanings).

Index

References are to *section numbers*, NOT *page numbers*.
A **bold face** number refers to the chief place where the topic in question is explained or discussed.

(References are to section numbers, NOT page numbers)

(References are to section numbers, NOT page numbers)

(References are to section numbers, NOT page numbers)